A PLUME BOOK

OPHELIA JOINED THE GROUP MAIDENS WHO DON'T FLOAT

Michael Schmelling

SARAH SCHMELLING has written for *The Washington Post*, *Newsweek*, *Spin*, *Real Simple*, *Variety*, and *McSweeney's Internet Tendency*, where her popular "Hamlet (Facebook News Feed Edition)" first appeared. She lives outside Washington, D.C., with her husband and son.

OPHELIA

JOINED THE GROUP
MAIDENS WHO DON'T FLOAT

CLASSIC LIT SIGNS ON TO FACEBOOK

SARAH SCHMELLING

A PLUME BOOK

PLUME
Published by the Penguin Group
Penguin Group (USA) Inc., 375 Hudson Street, New York, New York 10014, U.S.A. • Penguin Group (Canada), 90 Eglinton Avenue East, Suite 700, Toronto, Ontario, Canada M4P 2Y3 (a division of Pearson Penguin Canada Inc.) • Penguin Books Ltd., 80 Strand, London WC2R 0RL, England • Penguin Ireland, 25 St. Stephen's Green, Dublin 2, Ireland (a division of Penguin Books Ltd.) • Penguin Group (Australia), 250 Camberwell Road, Camberwell, Victoria 3124, Australia (a division of Pearson Australia Group Pty. Ltd.) • Penguin Books India Pvt. Ltd., 11 Community Centre, Panchsheel Park, New Delhi – 110 017, India • Penguin Group (NZ), 67 Apollo Drive, Rosedale, North Shore 0632, New Zealand (a division of Pearson New Zealand Ltd.) • Penguin Books (South Africa) (Pty.) Ltd., 24 Sturdee Avenue, Rosebank, Johannesburg 2196, South Africa

Penguin Books Ltd., Registered Offices: 80 Strand, London WC2R 0RL, England

First published by Plume, a member of Penguin Group (USA) Inc.

First Printing, September 2009
10   9   8   7   6   5   4   3   2   1

Illustrations on pp. 6–8, 221 by Nick Sung.

 REGISTERED TRADEMARK—MARCA REGISTRADA

LIBRARY OF CONGRESS CATALOGING-IN-PUBLICATION DATA

Schmelling, Sarah.
   Ophelia joined the group maidens who don't float : classic lit signs on to Facebook / Sarah Schmelling.
      p. cm.
   ISBN 978-0-452-29573-5
   1. Facebook (Electronic resource)—Parodies, imitations, etc.   2. Social networks—Humor.   3. Literature—Humor.   I. Title.
   PN6231.F24S36   2009
   302.30285—dc22

                                                                                        2009024113

Printed in the United States of America
Set in News Gothic BT
Designed by Spring Hoteling

Contents

OPHELIA
JOINED THE GROUP
MAIDENS WHO DON'T FLOAT

WILLIAM SHAKESPEARE'S ADMIRABLE, RIGHTEOUS, SINGULAR, AND INCOMPARABLE BOOKE CLUB GROUP

Globe-al

Basic Info

Type: Not, by any means, necessary

Description: TO MY MOST NOBLE, HONORABLE, PRAISE-
WORTHY, ADMIRABLE, AND ATTRACTIVE PURCHASERS. I MEAN
BRETHREN. HEREIN SHALL WE RESIDE FOR A SPELL AMONG
THE COMPANY OF SUCH GREAT MINDS AS TO

Oh, that's exhausting. Suffice it to say I was compelled to create this group in order to find everyone who is, let's say, borrowing liberally from my INESTIMABLE FOLIO OF CANONICAL MASTERPIECES (sorry, I just do that sometimes), and get you all together. It's the least I could do.

I mean, seriously. Those soliloquies in *Moby-Dick*? Sooo Hamlet and/or Othello, with maybe a little Shylock thrown in. Everyone from Pip in *Great Expectations* to freakin' Mr. Rochester in *Jane Eyre* mentions my plays, sometimes completely mangling my words in nineteenth-century middle-American dialect for humorous effect (thank you, Sir Clemens). Many people (*cough* Virginia Woolf *cough*) just quote me over and over again without attribution. I hear James Joyce even devoted a chapter of his giant novel to something called the "Hamlet theory," though do you have some sort of newfangled English? It looks like gobbledygook to me. The only people who don't seek me out are like Chaucer and Dante and those ancient Greeks. For whatever reason.

And then there are the titles. *The Sound and the Fury*? Mine. *Infinite Jest*? Mine. Proust, Nabokov, Steinbeck, and Agatha Christie all have titles that are me-inspired. *Brave New World*? Not just the title, but half the plot has to do with my work. Even Edgar Allan Poe named a character after my *Tempest*'s Prospero (though, not surprisingly, things didn't turn out well for him!). I'm like the star to every wandering bark, the arrow of every compass, the buzzard to every hawk and gillyflower . . . oh, I don't even know what I'm talking about half the time. I just run with it, creating some of the SEMINAL TOURS DE FORCE OF THE ENGLISH LANGUAGE. You're welcome.

To be (or not to be, ha!) . . . no, really, to be in this group, a few rules:

- You must mention my TREMENDOUS AND FATHOMLESS WORKS in some way. There are good ways and bad ways to go about this. For example, Holden Caulfield said about my play *Romeo and Juliet*, "I liked it a lot. There were a few things I didn't like about it, but it was quite moving, on the whole." This is not unequivocal praise, yet it will do. But then he went on to say that my main characters "get pretty annoying sometimes" and that he "felt much sorrier when old Mercutio got killed than when Romeo and Juliet did." While I'm glad that he found Mercutio a strong, three-dimensional character, it would kind of ruin the drama if I killed off the most important character midway through the play, wouldn't it? Also, way to give away the ending! Romeo and Juliet get "killed." A spoiler alert would help, Holden. Also, Mercutio wasn't that old.
- You must be either an author or a character of a "classic" work of literature. I'm not sure who decides on this "classic" thing. I believe it means as an author you must have suffered, toiled in obscurity, drank, battered yourself with heavy household items, contracted something on the English moors, done something embarrassing in public, had daddy issues, run off with a friend's wife or your own underage cousin, failed at writing Hollywood screenplays, or gone to your grave believing you were talentless and completely unloved. Of course, as I mentioned, "classic" is also a measure of how often you refer to me.
- If at all possible, somebody involved in your book had to have suffered a debilitating ailment, preferably a disease centered in the lungs or spread by body lice. Or they just died as many of my own characters did—from sadness, betrayal, grief, guilt, or, my favorite, the crazy.
- Your book, having appeared on numerous syllabi, has led at least one high school or college student to smack himself in the head, weep, hide under the bed, or reconsider his purpose in the universe.

All of you "classic" members of this group have been divided into networks by the topics you seem to enjoy most (which also not-so-coincidentally happen to be my pet interests): epic grandeur, the true misfortune that is love, our misguided youth, men and their need to fight one another and the cruel world, the horror in our souls, naughty naughtiness, those tragic fools of fortune, and playing around with language just to confuse people.

We're going to share your news feeds and biographical profiles, your groups and events, your games and quizzes, even things you thought nobody else could see (privacy settings, my arse). And I'll be chiming in every so often because, you know, I'm Shakespeare.

Please note that the news feeds you see here—unlike other news feeds you may have seen—

progress chronologically in time, like a book (except for a few books, you rascal Vonnegut). If this bothers you, try this: go to the bottom and read up. Also, note that all the works of literature in my orbit couldn't be included in this treatment of the "classics" because clearly that would be an insurmountable feat.

If you haven't seen a "news feed" elsewhere, it's a gathering of all the goings-on of one's large assembly of friends: what "groups" they've joined, that they've become "fans" of potatoes, that they sent mojitos to someone, or that they posted awkward photos of people they're purporting to care about. These feeds also contain "status updates," statements intended to convey what one is doing or thinking, but are more often made up of song lyrics or random displays of frustration or joy, or simply not written at all. This last option is understandable because people in this society are judged by the pithiness and novelty of their status updates. (And, yes, when you "comment" on a friend's status, we all judge you on that too.)

The following will not be tolerated here: Slurs, libel, slander, dullness, status updates that include the phrase "[Your name here] hates Mondays" or "Thank God it's Friday," emoticons used in an effort to mask one's lack of vocabulary, use of exclamation points that gives us the impression you've OD'd on cocaine and Pixy Stix, and abuse of texting acronyms. Unless you are a six-month-old infant or a little girl in a tickle fight, you are not really rolling on the floor laughing. If you are, you need to get up, go outside, and speak to another human being because there's something wrong with your sense of humor.

The following will be tolerated, in fact, expected: Obscenity, bawdiness, drollness, sly wit, bad puns, jokes about one's manhood, random song lyrics, histrionics, inside jokes, sudden mood swings, and references to things like pirates, cows, jousting, '80s keyboard-centric pop bands, monkeys, any of the later Beatles albums, Colin Firth, Kenny Rogers, house pets . . . I believe you get the idea.

But of course what makes a lot of these books classics is that their authors didn't conform to rules; they tried for something a little different and, in the process, made something great. Again, kind of like me. So feel free to maybe color outside the lines a little bit (spambots, that's not your cue to flood our pages with work-at-home and sexy cougar ads).

Enjoy reading. And always remember THE UNRIVALED, MASTERFUL MIND WHO STARTED IT ALL.

Yours,

William Shakespeare

1

Eve could use a bite to eat.

The Tales of Epic Proportion Network

Hamlet • *The Odyssey* • *The Canterbury Tales* • *Dante's Inferno* • *Paradise Lost* • *Beowulf*

Hamlet

NEWS FEED

- **Horatio** thinks he saw a ghost.

- **Hamlet** thinks it's annoying when your uncle marries your mother right after your dad dies.

- **The King** thinks Hamlet's annoying.

- **Laertes** thinks Ophelia can do better.

- **Hamlet's** father is now a **Zombie**.

- **The King** poked **The Queen**.

- **The Queen** poked **The King** back.

- **Hamlet** and **The Queen** are no longer friends.

- **Marcellus** is pretty sure something's rotten around here.

- **Hamlet** became a fan of **Daggers**.

- **Polonius** says Hamlet's crazy . . . crazy in love!

- **Rosencrantz, Guildenstern**, and **Hamlet** are now friends.

- **Hamlet** wonders if he should continue to exist. Or not.

- **Hamlet** thinks Ophelia might be happier in a convent.

- **Ophelia** removed "moody princes" from her **Interests**.

- **Hamlet** posted an **Event: A Play That's Totally Fictional and in No Way About My Family**.

- **The King** commented on Hamlet's play.

    "What is wrong with you?"

● **Polonius** thinks this curtain looks like a good thing to hide behind.

Polonius is no longer online.

Hamlet added **England** to the **Places I've Been** application.

● **The Queen** is worried about **Ophelia**.

● **Ophelia** loves flowers. Flowers flowers flowers flowers flowers. Oh, look, a river.

Ophelia joined the group **Maidens Who Don't Float**.

● **Laertes** wonders what the hell happened while he was gone.

The King sent **Hamlet** a **Goblet of Wine**.

● **The Queen** likes wine!

● **The King** likes . . . oh, crap.

The Queen, The King, **Laertes**, and **Hamlet** are now **Zombies**.

● **Horatio** says well, that was tragic.

● **Fortinbras, Prince of Norway,** says yes, tragic. We'll take it from here.

Denmark is now **Norwegian**.

The Odyssey

NEWS FEED

 Odysseus received a **notice**.

> "You haven't signed in for twenty years. Deactivate account?"

Penelope posted a **Survey: Is My Husband Still Alive?**

Zeus, Athena, and Telemachus: YES

Single Men of Ithaca: NO

● **Penelope** is weaving a shroud.

● **Penelope** unwound the shroud and is weaving it again.

✉ **Penelope** received **Marriage Proposals** from **Antinous**, **Agelaus**, **Amphinomus**, **Ctessippus**, **Demoptolemus**, **Elatus**, **Euryades**, **Eurymachus**, and **Peisandros**.

● **Penelope** will choose one of her suitors to marry when she's done weaving the shroud, which (woops!) she just unwound again.

 Hermes freed **Odysseus** from his captivity with the love-struck, gorgeous, immortality-promising nymph **Calypso**! He's free to go!

> **Hermes:** Yep, you can go.
>
> **Hermes:** Go ahead.
>
> **Hermes:** Any day now.

♪ **Odysseus** added "Homeward Bound" to his playlist.

● **Odysseus** is wondering where that giant wave came from.

> **Poseidon**: Maybe next time you stick a hot poker in someone's eye, you'll make sure his dad isn't the GOD OF THE SEA.

Odysseus received a **Shipwreck-Prevention Veil** from the **Goddess Ino**.

 Odysseus just found himself naked with the naked princess Nausicaa and her naked friends playing ball.

> **Odysseus:** I know this is strange, but I do really want to get home.

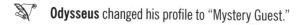 **Nausicaa** invited **Odysseus** to attend **Dinner at the Palace of The King and Queen aka The Parents**.

 **Odysseus** changed his profile to "Mystery Guest."

 The Blind Bard is singing a sad song about Odysseus and his big fight with Achilles.

> **The King:** I like our mystery guest, but why is he over there sobbing?

Odysseus was challenged to play **Original Olympic Sports**.

> **The King:** And wow! Look at him throw that discus.

 The Blind Bard is singing about the sack of Troy.

> **The King:** Sobbing again.

 **Odysseus** wrote on **The King's Wall**.

"I know I was hiding it pretty well, but I'm actually Odysseus."

Odysseus posted the album **Greek Isles Cruise, 1170 BC!**

There's me dragging my men back to the ship in the Land of the **Lotus-Eaters**.

There are my men being eaten by the **Cyclops**, and then me poking
his eye out with a stick. Poseidon was PISSED about that.

And there are my men tearing open a bag of wind. That didn't turn out well.

And, of course, **Circe** turning my men into pigs. She's crazy!

There we are visiting the land of the dead. Got to see **Tiresias** and **Mom**.
And **Ajax** and **Agamemnon**. If they're dead, they're there.

Oh, and **Sisyphus** with his rock. Man, that guy never gives up.

That's me filling my men's ears with beeswax to avoid hearing the **Sirens'** song. Though *I* heard it. Tempting!

And then **Scylla** gobbled up six more of my guys. There's **Charybdis**.

Then we made it through to the island of the **Sun**, though it didn't really matter because **Zeus** wiped out the rest of my men shortly after.

 Odysseus commented on his own album.

> *"So who wants to be on my crew back to Ithaca?"*

 Odysseus received a **Ride Home** from the **Phaeacians**.

Poseidon is letting the Phaeacians get almost all the way back before turning their boat to stone and sinking it to the bottom of the sea.

Athena is disguising herself as a shepherd to see how smart Odysseus is.

> **Odysseus:** Odysseus who?
>
> **Athena:** Ha! You're good. Now dress up in these old rags, and let's get killing.

Athena invited **Odysseus** to attend **The Old Swineherd's Hut**.

Athena invited **Telemachus** to attend **The Old Swineherd's Hut**.

> **Telemachus:** Dad?

Penelope's Small Fertile Square is overgrown with suitors! She can **buy a watering can**, **hose them down**, or **challenge them to feats of strength they'll never overcome**.

Penelope created a Test: **String a Bow, Shoot an Arrow Through Twelve Axes, and I'll Marry One of You Idiots**.

> **All The Suitors** failed! This test must be impossible!

Disguised Odysseus strung the bow, shot one arrow through twelve axes, and look, another arrow into a suitor's neck.

The Suitors joined **Odysseus** in a game of **Bloodbath**! **Odysseus** killed everyone. Compare your score.

Penelope says the house is covered with blood, the villagers are rampaging, and I think I just saw the goddess of wisdom hiding in the closet. You must be home, Odysseus.

> **Odysseus:** Come here, you.

Odysseus removed the **Places I Want to Visit** application.

Some People Odysseus May Know:

Homer Simpson
James Joyce
Helen of Troy
Zorba
Zeus
El Greco
Yanni

The Canterbury Tales
EVENT

Canterbury Pilgrimage and Storytelling Contest
Tell a Tale on the Way to Canterbury, Win Free Dinner!

Event Info

Host: Harry Bailey

Language: English (Middle)

Type: In goode fun

Time and Place

Date: All of April

Location: Tabard Inn, Southwerk, Engelond

Description:

Howdy, pilgrims! Has the Great Schism of Western Christianity or memories of the Black Death got you down? And how about this war? Doesn't it feel like it's been going on for a Hundred Years? Forget your troubles, and get going on a pilgrimage to the shrine of everyone's favorite martyr, Saint Thomas Becket. Join a group of folks with varying bathing habits and from all walks of life (seriously, it's like someone wants us to represent an entire society or something). Try your hand at religious devotion while also taking time to PARTY! Lord knows that even though we've got friars and monks around here, their godly dedication is highly questionable, so have fun!

We know that with Richard II still in power and blacksmithing prices the way they are, your purses might be tight. So, to make it a little more interesting this year (and to have people save $$ instead of robbing each other in their sleep, per usual), we're adding a Storytelling Contest component. Can you spin a good yarn? Telle tales to shorte with oure weye? Enter the Canterbury Pilgrimage First Annual

Storytelling Contest, and win not only a FREE MEAL on us but the honor of having one of the only tales remembered by high school students around the world (Miller, Wife of Bath, I'm looking at you).

Ol' Geoff Chaucer will be taking notes, and snarkily I bet, but I'll be your judge, and if you have a problem with that, you can pay for everything along the way! Make the stories lively and interesting, and it would be helpful if you could speak in decasyllable lines and match your rhetorical presentation to your social class. Oh, and rhyme.

Now lat us ryde, and herkneth what I seye! Who's with me?

Your Host, Harry Bailey

Confirmed Guests

The Knight, The Miller, The Wife of Bath, The Squire, The Yeoman, The Prioress, The Monk, The Friar, The Merchant, The Clerk, The Man of Law, The Franklin, The Pardoner, The Summoner, The Reeve, The Physician, The Host, Geoffrey Chaucer, A Bunch of Others Nobody Ever Remembers

Wall

The Knight wrote
I'll be there! I think I'll tell a story of Theseus, Duke of Athens, and Greek Gods like Mercury and Venus, and a big tournament between knights for the love of the fair Emelye. It'll be about destiny and fate and how the good and bad in life are all mixed together. I think I'll tell it in four parts, and it will be very noble, like me, a knight.

The Miller wrote
BORING! And noble, my ass. Actually, I should tell a story about asses. Big, plump, smelly asses. Like you all. And people kissing asses when they're stuck out windows and branding asses with hot pokers. Poker. Poke her. I don't even know them! Or him. Her.

The Reeve wrote
Drink much?

The Miller wrote
Much! What?

Chaucer wrote
I'm telling you right now, I'll just report these stories as I hear them. It's not my fault if some are moral and some are crass and full of fart jokes.

The Summoner wrote
Farts! Farts! Farts! Farts!

The Friar wrote
God, you're annoying.

The Summoner wrote
Huh, maybe my tale will be about an a-hole friar. Farts.

The Miller wrote
Oooh, and mine will be about an a-hole carpenter. Which has something to do with a reeve.

The Reeve wrote
And I'll tell one about an a-hole miller.

The Friar wrote
A-hole summoner.

The Summoner wrote
Fart! OH! Fart. Farty fart! And friars that come out of Satan's butt!

The Prioress wrote
Could we please tell tales about religion? Praise the Holy Virgin.

The Merchant wrote
Right. I'll tell one about people having sex in trees!

The Cook wrote
Cool! I'll tell one about this guy? Who parties a lot? And gambles? And knows this other guy whose wife is a hooker?

The Clerk wrote
I think I'll rip off Petrarch.

Chaucer wrote
Good thinking. There are going to be a lot of stories. We can't just completely make this stuff up.

The Wife of Bath wrote
I can tell a story about marriage, seeing that I've had five husbands. Oh, and my name is "The Wife."

The Miller wrote
FAAAARTS.

The Wife of Bath wrote
Pardon me!

The Pardoner wrote
Sure, but it's going to cost ya.

The Miller wrote
God save al the route! I am dronke, I knowe it by my soun.

The Host wrote
Oh, you always get untranslated when you drink too much. Wait, I want to hear from the Manciple.

The Knight wrote
Thc who?

The Summoner wrote
Fart! Stupid friars.

Chaucer wrote
Are we there yet?

The Wife of Bath's Tale

NEWS FEED

 The Wife joined the group **I Was a Preteen Bride**.

 The Wife is an active user of the **Choose a Good Husband!** application. She has been successful three out of five times.

 The Wife became a fan of **Using Sex to Lord over My Husband(s)**.

> **The Pardoner:** I'm getting married soon, and you're making me really nervous.
>
> **The Wife:** Calm down, and just listen to my tale, which I'll tell you in about six hundred more lines, but first let me describe what I put my husbands through and how they had to work so hard, and how the good ones were good because they were rich and old, and, oh, how I could get them to buy me things and I was always lying, lying, lying, and shifting the blame onto my husbands, oh, and my FOURTH husband, oh, the lout, and my fifth one, let me tell you what he did and what happened to him!

● **The Friar** would like **The Wife** to get to the Tale in The Wife of Bath's Tale.

The Tale in The Wife of Bath's Tale

NEWS FEED

● **A Lusty Knight** is roaming the countryside looking for maidenheads. Oh, found one!

● **King Arthur** thinks The Knight should be hanged.

● **The Queen** thinks that's kind of harsh.

● **The King** says fine, you decide what to do with him.

? **The Queen** challenged **The Knight** to the **Answer One Question and Your Life Will Be Saved** test. Test duration: one year. **The Knight** accepted the challenge with the reason, "I had no choice."

● **The Queen** says great!

The question is, **What do women want most?**

> **The Knight:** Oh, God.

● **The Knight** would really like to hear from everyone everywhere on this.

> **Woman #1**: It's honor.
>
> **Woman #2**: Pleasure.
>
> **Woman #3**: Nice clothes.
>
> **Woman #4**: Good sex.
>
> **Woman #5**: Having a lot of husbands.
>
> **Woman #6**: To be cosseted and flattered.
>
> **The Wife:** Oh, I totally agree with that one. Flattery and cosseting will do it every time.
>
> **Woman #7:** It's freedom to do exactly what we please. And to have no one call us on our mistakes. And for you to tell us we're smart.
>
> **Still More Women:** It's being told we're dependable and discreet.
>
> **The Wife:** Discreet! Ha! Remember the story of Midas? Let me tell it to you.

● **The Knight** still doesn't know the answer.

● **The Knight** is pretty depressed.

● **The Old Hag** knows the answer! Marry me, and I'll save your life.

> **The Knight:** Really? Sure.

? **The Knight** knows the answer! **Women want control over their husbands and lovers**.

● **The Old Hag** saved The Knight's life.

> **The Old Hag:** Great! Now marry me!

> **The Knight:** What's that?

 The Knight and **The Old Hag** are now married.

● **The Knight** is not a fan of his wife.

● **The Knight** can't stop weeping.

 The Old Hag challenged **The Knight** to a game of **Wife Swap**! Your wife can be either ugly and faithful or beautiful and a big whore.

● **The Knight** says it's up to you.

> **The Old Hag:** Really?
> **The Knight:** Sure.

 The Knight won the **Grand Prize**! A wife who's beautiful *and* faithful! All because he gave his wife **the power to decide for herself**, thus verifying the answer he searched for and the whole point of this story.

 **The Old Hag** changed her profile picture.

The Knight and the **Formerly Old Hag** are now living happily ever after.

● **The Wife** prays for husbands meek, young, and fresh in bed.

> **The Wife:** And grace to overbid them when we wed.

Quiz:

WHICH CIRCLE OF HELL ARE YOU IN?

by The Inferno*

ABANDON ALL HOPE, YE WHO ENTER HERE
Dante went to Hell and back to help you figure out where you belong. Answer these questions to find out!

1) **You have a crush on someone. You:**
   A) Write a short note to say hi while plugging your Web site where you can purchase hand-made cannoli from the comfort of YOUR OWN HOME!
   B) Put up a profile photo of your head pasted on someone else's body, and the head is someone else's too.
   C) Create an application to hack your crush's account and steal all his blocked personal information.
   D) Force him to take a **What's Your Favorite Position?** quiz, send him a naked photo of yourself, and post a note saying you're de-friending everyone else but him.

> —**If you chose A**, good news: you're only in the Opportunists' **Vestibule of Hell** (not even a Circle!). Thanks to your selfishness, you get to run around like a demented cat, chasing a banner you're never going to catch.
> —**If you chose B**, you're in the **Tenth Pocket of the Eighth Circle**—that's almost as low as you can go! Good luck hanging with the counterfeiters, Elvis impersonators, and other Falsifiers forced to deal with putrid odors, terrible thirst, filth, disease, and a loud shrieking noise, all in complete darkness.
> —**If you chose C**, welcome to the **Seventh Pocket of the Eighth Circle**. Here you'll join other Thieves in a pit of monstrous reptiles that act like living rope, binding up your hands and knotting themselves around your groin. Watch out for those lizards that fly at your neck, pierce your jugular vein, and make you burst into flames (though don't worry, if that happens, your soul will reform, and it can happen all over again!).

> —**If you chose D**, you belong in the **Second Circle**, reserved for carnal sinners. Try to stand up in a blinding tempest, forever resigned to not seeing light or anything, really, that isn't being whipped around in a frenzy.

2) **You're feeling bad about yourself. You:**

   A) Mask your inner pain by sending **Smiley Hugs** to people you don't really know or want to smile at. Or hug.
   B) Write a status update that says, "Jane Doe can't believe John went to virtual happy hour with 33 people that aren't me!"
   C) Write a status update that says, "Jane Doe doesn't see the point of breathing."
   D) Create a new application called **War on All Y'all**.

   > —**If you chose A**, you've made it to the **Sixth Pocket of the Eighth Circle**, full of fellow Hypocrites. Have fun wearing a lead robe and walking in circles. (We know, more circles! They've gone viral down here!)
   > —**If you chose B**, oooh, you're Sullen, and possibly a little Wrathful too. That puts you in the **Fifth Circle**, lying under the River Styx and making a horrific gargling noise and/or attacking other angry souls with rancid slime.
   > —**If you chose C**, you're in the **Middle Ring of the Seventh Circle**, where people are Violent to Themselves. Hope you enjoy being encased in a tree and fed upon by evil Harpies!
   > —**If you chose D**, you're in the **Outer Ring of the Seventh Circle**, you blood-lusting warmonger you. Say hi to your favorite warriors as you wallow in a river of boiling blood, while Centaurs threaten to shoot you full of arrows.

3) **It's your friend's birthday! You:**

   A) Write a tome on her **Wall** about how special and beautiful and smart she is, mainly just to get friend requests from other people.
   B) Send her a **Growing Bouquet of Daisies**, a **Cracking Egg**, a **Roast Turkey**, a **Christmas Tree Ornament**, six different **Friendship Symbols**, a **Cute Grin**, ten pieces of **Flair**, and some **Kitschy '80s Toys**.
   C) Send her a virtual chocolate cake, then go to the store and buy a giant, real chocolate cake and eat the whole thing right there in the parking lot. Then go back inside, sit down in the baking aisle, and scoop out and devour four containers of chocolate frosting with your fingers. Then bust open a bag of double-fudge cookies and shower them over your head, trying to catch pieces with your mouth.

D) Give her an application that, every time she logs on, automatically sends her friends dozens of inappropriate invites, viruses, **Thrown Snowballs**, and **Small Fertile Square** requests and then forces the same application on all of her friends' friends.

---**If you chose A**, oh, you Flatterer you, you're in the **Second Pocket of the Eighth Circle**. Just try and pull yourself out of that vat of excrement, which is a lot like the load of crap you've been dumping on people all these years.

---**If you chose B**, you're a Waster in **Circle Four**, pushing around huge rocks and locked in an eternal argument with a mob of Hoarders. Soon you'll be so full of rage your soul will be unrecognizable!

---**If you chose C**, yeah, you guessed it: you're a Glutton. You may only be in the **Third Circle**, but it'll seem like the Ninth as you lie in a rotting slush of putrefaction while a giant storm of garbage falls incessantly and Cerberus, the three-headed dog of Hell, stands over you, treating you like a giant, sewage-covered chew toy. You may have a touch of **Circle Seven** here as well, since you seem to be committing violence against both yourself and nature.

---**If you chose D**, well, you did it! You made it to the ultimate **Ninth Circle of Hell** by exemplifying Treachery against people who are bound to you by special ties. You've shown no capacity for love or human warmth, so sit back and enjoy eternity with your body trapped in a frozen lake, your head sticking out just enough that your tears fuse your eyelids together (though you might be able to catch a glimpse of nearby Satan chomping on Brutus, Cassius, and Judas Iscariot because, yeah, you're that far into the lowest realms of damnation). Wow. Forcing applications on your friends? You're really just the worst. Boo. BOOOOOO.

*This application was not developed by Dante, and frankly, he finds it degrading.

Paradise Lost

NEWS FEED

- **John Milton** is asserting Eternal Providence and justifying the ways of God to men! But he's totally modest about it.

- **John Milton** is attempting something unattempted yet in prose or rhyme!

- **The Serpent** created the group **Keeping the Tempted in Unattempted**.

- **God** removed **Satan** from his **Best Friends**.

- **Satan** added "Motivational Speaker" to his **Work Info**.

- **Satan** updated his **Favorite Quotations**.

   "Over? Did you say 'over'? Nothing is over until we decide it is! Was it over when the Germans bombed Pearl Harbor? Hell no!"

- **Satan** and **Beelzebub** are now fiends via the **Fiend Finder**.

- **Satan** and the fallen angels are magically erecting a temple called Pandemonium.

   Satan: What?

- **Beelzebub** heard God has a new world he's been working on.

- **Beelzebub** wonders how hard it would be to corrupt this race called Man.

   Satan: Oh, let me give it a whirl.

- **Satan** is now friends with **Sin**, **Death**, **Chaos**, **Confusion**, and **Discord**.

- **God** dedicated "Top of the World" to **Adam**.

- **God** hopes Man is preparing for Fall.

- **God** thinks Man will need a sacrifice, someone to die for his sins.

  > **Angels:** Um.
  >
  > **The Son:** Go ahead, make me a Man.

- **Satan** is in Limbo.

  > **Beelzebub:** How low can you go?

- **Satan** would like to make a Hell on Earth.

- **Adam** and **Eve** are new to **The World**.

- **Adam** and **Eve** joined the group **The Original Naturists**.

  > **Admin**: You must be friends with Adam and Eve to see their full profiles.
  >
  > **Adam:** No, we don't mind!
  >
  > **Eve:** Don't mind at all.

- **Eve** is in love with herself.

  > **Adam**: And Adam too!
  >
  > **Eve:** Right! And Adam too! You're my other half.
  >
  > **Adam**: Better half?
  >
  > **Eve:** Oh. Right again! I'm totally subservient to you!

- **Satan** has got to mess with these people.

- **The Angel Raphael** wrote on **Adam's Wall**.

God's Playlist

- "Always Look on the Bright Side of Life"
- "Almost Paradise"
- "Who Will Save Your Soul"
- "Who'll Stop the Rain"
- "It's Raining Men"
- "Man! I Feel Like a Woman!"
- "God Only Knows"
- "Dear God"
- "Stairway to Heaven"
- "Armageddon It"

"If you receive a message from Satan, or a weirdly smirking baby, or a frog or lizard of some kind, or someone who looks like Al Pacino, do NOT open it. It's infected."

- **Raphael** is explaining how the world was created.

- **Eve** would rather go tend her garden and have Adam explain it later because he's smarter than she is and it's nicer to hear it coming out of his mouth.

Adam posted a **Link**: **All About Eve**.

> **Adam:** I know she's my inferior. But she's just so beautiful.
>
> **Raphael:** But you know looks and sex aren't everything. And men are so much better than women anyway.

- **John Milton's** thoughts on Eve have nothing to do with his woman troubles.

- **Eve** would like some time alone.

> **Adam:** Fine, but look out for our mortal enemy! And don't seek temptation or fall into deception! And be obedient, and keep your virtue, and remember you're the mother of all mankind!
>
> **Eve:** Will do! Hey, there's a talking snake.
>
> **The Serpent:** Trouble in Paradise?

 The Serpent sent **Eve** an **Apple**.

> **Eve:** Hmm.
>
> **The Serpent:** Oh, I had one the other day. I'm fine. That's why I can talk.

- **Eve** could use a bite to eat.

- **The Earth** is shuddering and sighing because all is lost.

> **Eve:** Damn! That's a good apple.

● **Eve** thinks Adam should have some of this.

> **Eve**: Adam?
>
> **Adam**: Sorry, I was just feeling cold horror running through my veins and watching these flower petals shrivel up and die.

● **Adam** might as well eat it too because they're already screwed.

● **Eve** is having the best sex ever with Adam.

> **Eve:** Oh, right. It's lustful, bad sex.
>
> **Adam**: Yes, bad. Very bad.

 Adam sent **Eve** a **Fig Leaf**.

? **Adam** challenged **Eve** to a **Quiz: What's Changed Now That You Did What You Did?** Pick all that apply.

> We now feel shame.
>
> We now feel hate, anger, and jealousy.
>
> We have to go hunt for our food.
>
> You get to feel the pain of childbirth.
>
> We no longer get perfect weather because the earth has changed its axis.
>
> We'll never have a peaceful night's sleep again.
>
> Oh, and we're no longer immortal.

Eve answered: **All of the Above**. Though you forgot "Women and men will now drive each other crazy." You know, you should have never let me go off on my own.

> **Adam**: Oh, it's my fault? Really? Yes, maybe it's my mistake to think you could be trusted. Ungrateful apple-eater.
>
> **Eve:** God! Let's just argue about this for the rest of time.

> **Adam**: Fine!
>
> **Eve**: Fine!

● **God** is wondering what's going on down there.

> **Adam**: She made me do it!

● **Adam** says you know, I never asked to be created. I feel like a monster.

> ✴ **Mary Shelley** likes this.

🎀 **Eve** sent **Adam** a **Wrecking-the-Whole-Human-Race Apology**. See what other apologies have opened up! Collect them all.

🎀 **Adam** sent **Eve Forgiveness**.

✉ **Michael the Archangel** sent **Adam** and **Eve** an **Eviction Notice**.

● **Adam** wonders if we could give God a forwarding address?

📷 **Michael the Archangel** posted the album **Panorama of Human History**.

> Tagged in this album: **Cain** and **Abel**, **Enoch**, **Moses**, **Joshua**, **David**, **Noah**, the **Tower of Babel**, **Ham**

● **Adam** is wow, not very proud of my offspring.

> **Michael the Archangel**: But God's also going to send his Son to triumph over Satan and enter into glory.
>
> **Adam**: Awesome. So what should we do now?

🎵 **Michael the Archangel** dedicated "Faith" to **Adam**.

● **Eve** wonders what she missed while she was sleeping.

> **Adam**: Don't worry, I'll fill you in.

Adam gave **Eve** his **Hand**.

> **Eve**: I'm sorry, I guess I felt sympathy for the devil.
>
> **Adam**: Well, you can't always get what you want.
>
> **Eve**: No, I can't get no satisfaction.
>
> **Adam**: But can you gimme shelter?
>
> **God**: Hey, you, get off of my cloud.
>
> **God**: Heh.

Dante and Milton Play Scrabulific!

```
      | S |   |
      | A |   |
S | A | T | A | N
A |   | A |   |
T |   | N |   |
A |   |   |   |
N |   |   |   |
```

SMACK TALK!

Milton: This is getting a little repetitive, don't you think?

Dante: I don't know. Our Satans are quite different, really.

Milton: Oh, right, my Satan is on a double word score.

Dante: No, I mean my Satan, in my INFERNO, is much scarier than yours.

Milton: I like a Satan with a little personality though.

Dante: That's where we differ.

Twenty Questions for the Author of Beowulf

by Unknown (Translated by Seamus Heaney)

By popular demand (would you all stop tagging me already?), I've cut and pasted these questions in a note and written my answers. Enjoy!

1. WHERE WERE YOU BORN? Anglo-Saxonia Land? Not sure what they're calling it these days.

2. IF YOU COULD BE ANOTHER PERSON BESIDES YOURSELF, WOULD YOU BE FRIENDS WITH YOU? What? And MY form of English is confusing?

3. DO YOU STILL HAVE YOUR TONSILS? I'm happy to still have my head.

4. WHO DO YOU MISS THE MOST? Ol' Shield Shiefson. A fun guy.

5. WHAT KIND OF ACCENT DO YOU HAVE? It's pretty much Early West Saxon. Though my a's sometimes sound Northumbrian.

6. WHAT DO YOU DO FOR FUN? Recite my poem. Collect pelts.

7. DO YOU USE SARCASM? I try, but it's a little hard to convey through hyphenated Old English in alliterative verse.

8. FAVORITE "ETHNIC" FOOD? Holy Roman Empiric.

9. WHAT ARE YOU WEARING? My casual-Fridays helmet, a dead animal, and those boots with the crisscross straps up the sides.

10. WHAT KIND OF MUSIC DO YOU LIKE? Hmm. I like the harp that accompanies me while I tell my stories. Those people who sing in mead halls. The occasional pan flute.

11. WHAT IS THE FIRST THING YOU NOTICE ABOUT PEOPLE? Their eyes. And whether they're trying to kill me.

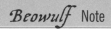

12. ROLLING STONES OR BEATLES? Are those things forms of punishment or something you eat?

13. WHAT'S YOUR RELIGION? Christian with a hint of Pagan.

14. HUGS OR KISSES? No idea what you're referring to.

15. WHO INSPIRES YOU? For my writing, I'm going to say God . . . since nobody wrote anything in English before me. Ever.

16. WHEN WAS THE LAST TIME YOU CRIED? That thing that infants do? Well, I guess when I was an infant.

17. WHAT ARE YOU LISTENING TO RIGHT NOW? The women cooking something over the fire that appears to still be squealing.

18. WHAT IS THE FARTHEST YOU HAVE BEEN FROM HOME? Just past that hill over there. But I know a guy who's been to Finland.

19. FAVORITE DESSERT? Key Lime Cheesecake.

20. WHAT DO YOU DO TO BE CREATIVE? I drink a lot and tell the same story over and over again to people and hope that something sticks.

COMMENT

King Canute the Great: Awesome answers, dude. And I love your poem. It really sheds some light on our people.

J. R. R. Tolkien: I'm so glad to get the chance to learn more about you! I have so many questions. I guess, first, is the manuscript we have solely your work? Or was it the result of oral tradition being put on paper after being told for many years?

Unknown: Man, you're going to make the Academics go CRAZY. I'm not going to go there.

J. R. R. Tolkien: What does the dragon represent?

Unknown: A dragon. Don't you have dragons?

Geoffrey Chaucer: I'm just so happy someone whose work is so OLD has been rediscovered. Makes my work seem young and fresh.

William Shakespeare: Hear, hear!

Homer: Um, HELLO?

Seamus Heaney: Unknown, I'm wondering what you think of that *Beowulf* film.

Unknown: I like it, though I think some creative license was applied. I mean no one wears those funky headbands anymore. So ninth century.

King Canute the Great: What I don't understand is, why doesn't Naked Angelina Jolie show up in my copy of the poem?

Unknown: I keep getting asked this. For the record, Grendel's mother was a hideous beast. In fact, I believe I called her a "monstrous hell-bride" and "that swamp-thing from hell."

King Canute the Great: Right. Angelina Jolie.

Unknown: No. Grendel's mother was a monster and not, in fact, Angelina Jolie.

King Canute the Great: How can I get myself a Naked Angelina Jolie?

Unknown: And you wonder why I stay Unknown.

2

Elizabeth threw a sheep at Mr. Darcy.

The Love and Other Difficulties Network

Shakespeare's Comedies • Pride and Prejudice • Jane Austen • Jane Eyre • Wuthering Heights • Anna Karenina • The Scarlet Letter

Shakespeare's Comedies
NEWS FEED

Now with *The Winter's Tale*!
(Problem plays not included)

 Antipholus of Syracuse, Orlando, Oliver, The King of Navarre, Berowne, Longaville, Dumaine, Lucentio, Viola, Olivia, Gratiano, Proteus, and **Claudio** fell in **Love at First Sight!** with **Luciana, Rosalind, Celia, The Princess, Rosaline, Maria, Katherine, Bianca, Orsino, Cesario, Nerissa, Silvia,** and **Hero.**

 Oliver, Orlando, Duke Senior, and **Duke Frederick** are in **Blood Feuds.**

 Egeon, Emilia, two Antipholi, Viola, and **Sebastian** were **Shipwrecked.**

● **King Leontes** suspects his wife is cheating.

● **Page** thinks his wife wouldn't cheat.

● **Ford** thinks his wife just might.

 Silvius, Don Armado, Gremio, Hortensio, Orsino, Bassanio, Caius, Fenton, Proteus, Valentine, Thurio, Florizel, Helena, Demetrius, and **Hermia** sent **Love Hugs** to **Phoebe, Jaquenetta, Bianca, Olivia, Portia, Anne Page, Julia, Silvia, Perdita, Demetrius, Hermia,** and **Lysander.**

● **Katherine the Shrew** has no Love Hugs. Or friends.

● **Antipholus** and **Dromio of Syracuse** are fleeing to an abbey.

● **Rosalind, Orlando, Celia, Touchstone, Hermia, Lysander, Demetrius,** and **Helena** are fleeing to the woods.

● **Falstaff** is plotting to seduce Mistresses Page and Ford.

● **Mistresses Page** and **Ford** are plotting to embarrass Falstaff.

- Caius and Evans are plotting to get back at the Host.

- Oberon is plotting to get back at Titania.

- Puck is looking for a flower with magic love juice he can spread on people's eyelids.

 Orlando challenged Charles to a Fight!

 Sir Andrew and Caius challenged Cesario and Evans to Duels.

- Oberon and Titania are fighting over a small Indian boy.

- Beatrice and Benedick are engaging in witty repartee.

- Katherine would like to injure Petruchio.

- Portia is waiting for a suitor to pick one out of three caskets.

- Touchstone, Costard, Feste, and Clown are being clowns.

- Slender is being an idiot.

- Adriana, Luciana, Sir Andrew, Sir Toby, Olivia, Antonio of Illyria, The Duke of Venice, Bassanio, Gratiano, Slender, Caius, Puck, and Claudio mistook Antipholus of Syracuse, Sebastian, Viola, Portia, Nerissa, two little boys, Lysander, and Margaret for Antipholus of Ephesus, Viola, Sebastian, men, Anne Page, Demetrius, and Hero.

- Christopher Sly is a fool who thinks he's a lord.

- Rosalind fooled Orlando into wooing her.

- Maria fooled Malvolio into dressing in yellow stockings and crossed garters, acting haughtily, smiling constantly, and refusing to explain why.

- Puck confused Demetrius and Lysander by mimicking their voices.

- Sebastian agreed to marry Olivia even though he has no idea who she is.

- Bassanio picked the right casket.

- **Claudio** left Hero at the altar.

- **Rosalind, Viola, Portia, Nerissa, a page boy, Celia, The King of Navarre, Longaville, Dumaine, Lucentio, Hortensio, Tranio, Feste, Jessica, Julia, Ford, Falstaff, the children, Polixenes,** and **Camillo** changed their profile pictures. They are now **men, a woman, a shepherdess, Muscovites, a Latin teacher, a music teacher, Lucentio, a priest, two pages, a man named Brooke, a servant's fat aunt, ghosts and monsters,** and **two just disguised people.**

- **Valentine** was banished, taken by outlaws, and made to be their king.

- **Antipholus of Ephesus** was locked in a cellar.

- **Hermione** was thrown in prison.

- **Malvolio** was locked in a small, dark room.

- **Perdita** was abandoned as a baby and raised by a shepherd.

- **Falstaff** was hidden in a basket, taken out with the laundry, and dumped in the river.

- **The Host's** horses were stolen.

- **Bottom's** head was transformed into that of an ass.

- **Antigonus** was killed by a bear.

- **The Princess, Rosaline, Maria,** and **Katherine** are pretending to be each other.

- **Hero** is pretending to be dead.

- **Tranio** and **Lucentio** are trying to get an old man to pretend to be Lucentio's father.

- **Mistress Quickly** is pretending to be the fairy queen.

- **Titania** IS the fairy queen.

- **Orsino** says if music can keep love alive he'd like it to continue.

- **Jaques** says it's like we're all on a big stage, acting out roles.

- **Katherine** says if she's like a wasp, Petruchio should be wary of her sting.

- **Shylock** asks if you pricked him, wouldn't he bleed? Also, for a pound of flesh.

- **Portia** doesn't think you can strain the quality of mercy.

- **Lysander** doesn't think the road of love is ever smooth.

- **Puck** thinks mortals be a bunch of fools.

- **Vincentio** is shocked to see Tranio pretending to be Lucentio.

- **Falstaff** is being terrified, pinched, and burned by children dressed as ghouls.

- **Portia** and **Nerissa** are mad that Bassanio and Gratiano gave away their rings, even if it was to Portia and Nerissa in disguise.

- **Julia**, as Sebastian, gave the ring Proteus gave her to Silvia, saying it's from Proteus.

- **Lysander** was mistakenly given a love potion and fell in love with Helena, who loves Demetrius, who usually loves Hermia, who challenged Helena to a fight.

- **Silvia** was abandoned in the woods, taken by outlaws, saved by Proteus, attacked by Proteus, and saved by Valentine, who then offered her to Proteus.

- **Julia** has now passed out.

- **Egeon, Emilia, Antipholus of Ephesus, Antipholus of Syracuse, two Dromios, Viola, Sebastian, King Leontes,** and **Perdita** were reunited with long-lost family members.

- **Proteus** realized he loves Julia after all.

- **Puck** got the love juice straightened out.

- **Valentine** got clemency for the outlaws.

- **Antonio** didn't have to give up his pound of flesh.

- **Ford** apologized for being a jealous guy.

- **Katherine** won the "Most Tamed" contest.

- **Claudio** thought he was marrying a mystery person, but really she's Hero.

- **Bottom**, **Quince**, **Flute**, **Snout**, **Snug**, and **Starveling** performed a terrible version of Pyramus and Thisbe.

- **Egeon** was pardoned.

- **Duke Frederick** found God and returned the throne to Duke Senior.

- **Lorenzo** and **Jessica** found out they'll inherit Shylock's estate.

- **Hymen,** the God of Marriage, made a guest appearance.

- **Malvolio** was released from the dark room.

- **Petruchio** asked Kate to kiss him.

- **Hermione** came back to life.

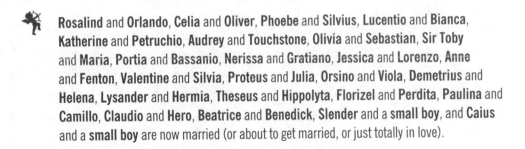 **Rosalind** and **Orlando**, **Celia** and **Oliver**, **Phoebe** and **Silvius**, **Lucentio** and **Bianca**, **Katherine** and **Petruchio**, **Audrey** and **Touchstone**, **Olivia** and **Sebastian**, **Sir Toby** and **Maria**, **Portia** and **Bassanio**, **Nerissa** and **Gratiano**, **Jessica** and **Lorenzo**, **Anne** and **Fenton**, **Valentine** and **Silvia**, **Proteus** and **Julia**, **Orsino** and **Viola**, **Demetrius** and **Helena**, **Lysander** and **Hermia**, **Theseus** and **Hippolyta**, **Florizel** and **Perdita**, **Paulina** and **Camillo**, **Claudio** and **Hero**, **Beatrice** and **Benedick**, **Slender** and a **small boy**, and **Caius** and a **small boy** are now married (or about to get married, or just totally in love).

- **Puck** says if all of this bothered you, don't sue us, it was just a dream.

Quiz:

SHAKESPEARE COMEDY OR THREE'S COMPANY?

1. A man tricks two women into being locked up with him in a cabin to determine which one is secretly in love with him.

2. Two women trick a man into going to the woods to be humiliated for his actions.

3. A man wants to woo Greedy Gretchen.

4. A man wants Mistress Quickly to help him woo a woman.

5. Everyone goes down to the Garter Inn to discuss what's going on.

6. Everyone goes down to the Regal Beagle to discuss what's going on.

7. A group of people misunderstands a doctor and thinks a woman is dying.

8. A woman makes a group of people think she's dead.

9. A woman disguises herself as a man and convinces a man to practice his wooing techniques on her.

10. A man pretends to like men and convinces his landlord to give him lessons on wooing women.

11. A man overhears a conversation and thinks his fiancée is cheating on him.

12. A man overhears a conversation and thinks a nun is in love with him.

13. A man's tryst is revealed when he's afflicted by a plant that causes itching.

14. A man falls in love with a woman after being afflicted by a plant that causes desire.

15. A woman wakes up with an ass-headed man.

16. A man wakes up with Mr. Roper.

Answer Key:

Three's Company: *1, 3, 6, 7, 10, 12, 13, 16*

Shakespeare: *2, 4, 5, 8, 9, 11, 14, 15*

Pride and Prejudice

NEWS FEED

 Mrs. Bennet posted a news story.

> *Everyone knows every rich, single man wants a wife.*

 Mrs. Bennet hacked all of her daughters' accounts.

 Mrs. Bennet changed her daughters' **Relationship Statuses** to "SINGLE REALLY SINGLE!"

 Mrs. Bennet wonders if the rich, single Mr. Bingley would want one of her daughters for a wife. Like Jane? Or Lizzy? Or maybe Lydia? Or Mary? Or Kitty? Or maybe Jane?

● **Mr. Bennet** wonders if he could drink his tea.

 The Bennets played **Line-Dancing in Regency England**.

 Mr. Bingley invited **Jane** to dance.

 Mr. Bingley invited **Jane** to dance.

 Mr. Bingley invited **Jane** to dance.

 Mr. Bingley and **Jane** are now in a relationship.

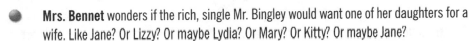 **Elizabeth** found **Mr. Darcy** through the **Some People You May Know** tool.

> *Mr. Darcy is new to Hertfordshire. Suggest friends for Mr. Darcy.*

Bridget Jones: Me! Me! Me! Me!

Mr. Darcy: I don't need friends.

❀ **Elizabeth** sent **Happy Feelings** to **Mr. Darcy**.

Mr. Darcy: I don't receive gifts from people who are obviously beneath me.

Elizabeth: Yes, and it must be hard to see with your head so far up your butt.

Mr. Darcy changed his privacy settings.

Jane was invited to attend **Dinner at the Bingleys'**.

Mrs. Bennet blocked **Jane's** access to a carriage despite the torrential rainstorm.

Jane received a **notice** that her account is now infected.

Jane is just resting here at the Bingleys' house until she recovers.

Mrs. Bennet has 100 percent compatibility with **Mother Nature** on **How to Get These Kids Together**.

Mr. Collins became heir to the **Bennet Estate**.

Mr. Collins sent a friend request to **Elizabeth**.

Mr. Collins sent a **Bouquet of Tulips** to **Elizabeth**.

Mr. Collins sent a **Martini** to **Elizabeth**.

Mr. Collins sent a **Chai Cream Frappuccino** to **Elizabeth**.

Mr. Collins sent an **Awkward Hug** to **Elizabeth**.

Mr. Collins sent an **Engagement Ring** to **Elizabeth**.

Elizabeth is ignoring **Mr. Collins**.

Mr. Collins and **Charlotte Lucas** are now married.

> **Elizabeth**: What the?
>
> **Mr. Darcy**: Hmm, maybe I should marry you.

Elizabeth threw a sheep at **Mr. Darcy**.

Lydia, Kitty, and **Elizabeth** became fans of **Men in Military Uniform Like Mr. Wickham**.

Mr. Wickham sent **Lydia, Kitty**, and **Elizabeth** a lot of **Hot Air** and a **Wad of Hooey**.

Mr. Darcy wrote on **Elizabeth's Wall**.

> *"So all those reasons why you hate me—that you think I've kept Jane and Bingley apart and that I did crappy things to Mr. Wickham—they're not true."*

Elizabeth wrote on **Mr. Darcy's Wall**.

> *"What about the part where you're a pompous ass?"*

Mr. Darcy wrote on **Elizabeth's Wall**.

> *"There is that."*

● **Elizabeth** hates him! She hates him! Though she might also love him.

● **Lady Catherine de Bourgh** cannot believe Darcy could love such a grungy little crumpet.

● **Mr. Bennet** is wondering who this Darcy person is again.

▨ **Lydia** was tagged in her own album, **I'm in Brighton Looking at All the Very Cute Soldiers . . . Is Anyone Paying Attention?**

● **Mrs. Bennet** is WEDDINGS!

● **Lydia** was **Kidnapped!** by **Mr. Wickham**. She lost 100 points and possibly her dignity.

● **Mr. Darcy** is secretly paying for Lydia and Mr. Wickham's wedding.

● **Mr. Darcy** is saving the Bennet family honor.

● **Mr. Darcy** is encouraging Mr. Bingley to propose to Jane.

Ten Random Things about Fitzwilliam Darcy

1. I'm in love with Elizabeth Bennet even though her mother is barking mad.

2. I have an irrational fear of needlepoint, and it's EVERYWHERE.

3. I can't stand to hear people whistle.

4. I tend to mask my insecurities with haughtiness.

5. Yes, this giant collar is itchy.

6. I'm allergic to kiwi.

7. My girl cousins used to put a bonnet on me and call me Poncey.

8. I'm not comfortable with my position as an archetype.

9. I have a tattoo of the Chinese symbol for "rooster" on my left bicep. Yes, there's a story there.

10. Deep down, I just want to be loved.

 Mr. Darcy posted a **Link**: **My Immense Family Estate**.

 Elizabeth upgraded her thoughts on **Mr. Darcy**.

 Elizabeth wrote on **Mr. Darcy's Wall**.

"I'm sorry I was prejudiced."

Mr. Darcy wrote on **Elizabeth's Wall**.

"I'm sorry I was proud."

 Mr. Bennet accepted **Daughter's Hand** requests from **Mr. Bingley** and **Mr. Darcy**.

Mr. Bennet couldn't have parted with Lizzy for anyone less worthy.

Mrs. Bennet's head might just explode.

 Jane and **Mr. Bingley** are now married.

 Elizabeth and **Mr. Darcy** are now married.

> **Mr. Bennet**: Isn't this wonderful?
>
> **Mrs. Bennet**: Yes, wonderful, but we do have more daughters you know.

 Mrs. Bennet posted a **Link**: **Kitty and Mary's profiles on Match.com**.

Jane Austen
PROFILE

Basic Information

Birthday: December 16, 1775

Hometown: Chawton

Personal Information

Interests: Class struggle, the role of women in early-nineteenth-century Britain, not conforming
to one genre, witty rejoinders, archery

Wall

 Notice from Admin:

You have 4,537 pending friend requests.

 Jane Austen wrote on **Cassandra Austen's Wall**.

*"Cassandra! Can you help me with this? I don't know why all these people want to be
my friend. Is it even possible to know 4,537 people?"*

 Jane Austen is trying to get some work done!

Cassandra Austen: Dear Jane, you're hugely popular. There are groups here with
thousands of people who just want to talk about you.

Jane Austen: I saw that! I also see people are setting up profile pages for "me," but
they have me living in places called "Buffalo Grove" or "Missouri" and they say my
friends include Michelangelo and Napoleon Bonaparte.

Cassandra Austen: It's confusing, I know.

Bridget Jones: Ugh. Can understand. MY day has been day of horror too. Turkey Curry Buffet. And got on M6 instead of M1 and drove halfway to Birmingham. Stupid f—kwit.

Jane Austen: And what's up with her?

 Jane Austen would rather not tell everyone what's on her mind.

Jane Austen: Actually, I'm also wondering about all these "book clubs."

Cassandra Austen: There are millions of people all over the world who spend a great deal of time discussing your books.

Jane Austen: Really? What do they discuss?

Emma Thompson: How about which sister in *Sense and Sensibility* is more like Jane herself? Or, yourself.

Karen Joy Fowler: And why isn't Mr. Knightley more appealing?

Bridget Jones: And which of your characters is the most annoying?

Colin Firth: And who's a better Darcy, Matthew Macfadyen or Colin Firth?

Elizabeth Bennet: Why is Lady Catherine so mean?

William Shakespeare: And why do people keep talking about your work when they could be talking about mine?

 Jane Austen is writing.

Jane Austen: All right, so I can see how there may be a lot to discuss in my books. But why so much attention to me? My life? It's really not that interesting.

Anne Hathaway: But why didn't you marry? And were you ever in love?

William Shakespeare: And who were your influences?

Charlotte Brontë: And who's your agent?

Keira Knightly: What movie adaptation is most realistic?

Karen Joy Fowler: And which was your favorite book?

Mrs. Bennet: Why are many of your mother characters silly and idiotic?

● **A Lawyer** responded to that statement.

Rochester suggested a friend for **Jane**: his secret wife, **Bertha**. He thinks she may know Bertha too.

> **Rochester**: You know, from all the fiendish attic laughter, and the ripping your veil to shreds in the middle of the night, oh, and that whole bed-on-fire incident.

● **Rochester** can easily explain all of this. If Bertha could just stop trying to wrench his head off his body.

● **Rochester** hopes Jane can understand.

● **Jane** is getting the hell out of —shire.

Jane is adding to her **Family Tree**! Not only did **Mary**, **Diana**, and **St. John Rivers** rescue her from homelessness and starvation, they're actually related too!

Jane received a **Large Inheritance**.

St. John invited **Jane** to be an **Exciting Missionary in Exotic India**. And to be his wife!

Jane was sent a **Haunting Voice** floating through the air.

> **Rochester**: Jane! Jane! Jane!
>
> **Jane**: Where are you? I am coming! Wait for me! Oh, I will come!
>
> **St. John**: What?

● **Jane** is going to Thornfield!

The Innkeeper posted a news story.

> *Thornfield burned to ground by crazy attic-wife. Crazy attic-wife dead. Rochester injured but okay and living at Ferndean.*

● **Jane** is going to Ferndean!

?   **Jane** suggested a new answer for the **How Would You Snag a Byronic Hero?** quiz.

> *"Find out that he's blind, return to him months later after running away in the middle of the night and living with another family, pretend to be a servant, make him feel slightly crazy, then feel pure joy as he realizes you're there and you're you."*

● **Rochester** was blinded by love! (And also by his mad wife who set his house on fire.)

● **Rochester** was blind but now he sees.

> **Jane**: Reader, I married him.

Quiz:

HOW WOULD YOU SNAG A BYRONIC HERO?

Choose your **MOST** favorite to **LEAST** favorite methods:

—Wander listlessly down a lane, distracting him so he falls off a horse.

—Act weirdly polite while he hurls insults, says he doesn't care you're there, completely ignores you, and says nasty things to a little girl.

—Hide in the corner as he woos high society women.

—Engage in witty repartee.

—Completely ignore those bizarre noises from the third floor.

—Grow up with him, treat him like crap for years, marry someone else, swoon a lot, die, then haunt him till his dying day.

Wuthering Heights
NEWS FEED

 Lockwood commented on his own photo in the album **Yorkshire Moors**.

> *"It's so gorgeous here and relaxing, and everyone is so nice!"*

 Lockwood sent **Heathcliff** a **Firm Handshake** and a **Pleasant Smile**.

 Heathcliff sent **Lockwood** a **Frightening Blizzard**, a **Pack of Snarling Dogs**, and **No Help**.

 Lockwood has been **Haunted**! **Phantom Cathy** is tapping on his window with a tree branch! **Let her in, kick her in the face,** or **just scream like a banshee till she goes away**.

● **Lockwood** is screaming like a banshee.

> **Heathcliff**: You're a fool, and why are you here in the first place? Away with you!
>
> **Heathcliff**: So did she say anything about me?

 Lockwood posted a **Link: Travel Tipster Review of Wuthering Heights**.

 Lockwood is now friends with **Nelly Dean**.

 Nelly and **Lockwood** played a game of **Flashback! 1760s Edition**.

> *Put your news feed in a time machine, and see what was going on back when King George III was still sane, Haydn was all the rage, and we couldn't wait for the development of the steam engine.*

Nelly's Flashback
NEWS FEED

 Mr. Earnshaw sent a **Lil' Heathcliff** to his family using **Kids Picked off the Street as Gifts**.

Lil' **Heathcliff** is now friends with **Catherine**.

 Mr. Earnshaw changed his Top Son from **Hindley** to **Heathcliff**.

 Mr. Earnshaw invited **Hindley**, **Heathcliff**, and **Catherine** to attend **My Funeral, Which Should Pretty Much Throw Everything into Chaos**.

 Hindley became a fan of **SWEET REVENGE**.

 Heathcliff became a fan of **YOU DON'T KNOW SWEET REVENGE UNTIL YOU SEE THIS KIND OF REVENGE REVENGE**.

 Hindley is now married.

 Hindley added **Hareton** to his **Family Tree** as his son.

 Hindley added "Alcoholic Widower with a Penchant for Guns" to his **About Me**.

 Catherine is upgrading her family! She's trading her violent brother and grungy stable-boy friend for a more normal family, **The Lintons**.

 Edgar Linton added "wooing a girl even though she seems obsessively in love with her adopted brother" to his **Activities**.

 Edgar and **Catherine** are now engaged.

 Catherine wrote on **Nelly's Wall**.

> *"I'm going to marry Edgar because he's handsome and pleasant and really rich. Marrying Heathcliff would be degrading."* **[Click to continue reading.]**

> *"Even though, of course, my love for Heathcliff is like the strength of eternal rocks and he's the only reason I live and he's more myself than I am."*

Nelly thinks Heathcliff probably should have clicked to continue reading.

Heathcliff played **Run Away!** He won 500 points for escaping Wuthering Heights, then lost 20,000 points for coming back just to torture everyone.

Catherine wrote on **Heathcliff's Wall**.

> *"So glad to see you here! You look exactly the same except for those expensive clothes, the lack of feces in your hair, and that demented gleam in your eye."*

Heathcliff is URGH revenge revenge revenge and . . .

Isabella Linton flirted with **Heathcliff**! She winked, batted her eyelashes, and threw herself on the floor in front of him.

Heathcliff added the **Marrying Someone Out of Pure Spite** application.

Catherine is refusing to eat.

Catherine is running around weeping in the rain.

Catherine is ranting hysterically, swooning, collapsing, giggling, sobbing, and sitting for hours next to open windows while pregnant during winter.

Catherine gave birth to Young Cathy.

Catherine's account was infiltrated by a virus due to **Activities Always Fatal for Gothic Heroines**.

Heathcliff sent a **Haunt Me Forever** request to **Dead Catherine**.

Hindley sent a **Knife-Gun** to **Heathcliff**.

Hindley woops.

Heathcliff now owns **Wuthering Heights**.

Isabella added **London** to her **Cities I Should Flee to Because I'm Pregnant and Living in a Horror House with a Bunch of Psychotics**.

Isabella named her son **Linton Heathcliff** via the **Emily Brontë's Brain-Numbingly Similar Name Generator** application.

 Linton changed his profile to **Frail Wimpy Teenager**.

 Linton received a **Live with Me** command from his father, **Heathcliff**, followed swiftly by a **Marry This Girl So I, I Mean You, Can Inherit Her House** command.

 Linton and **Young Cathy** are now married.

● **Linton** says wow! What a great wife I have, and now I own her house cause . . .

 Heathcliff now owns **Cathy's** house via the **Fathering a Frail Wimpy Son** application.

● **Heathcliff** stopped eating.

● **Heathcliff** is seeing Catherines everywhere.

 **Heathcliff** became a fan of **Necrophilia**.

● **Heathcliff** is going to go watch Six Feet Under.

 Young Cathy and **Haroton** are playing **Kissin' Cousins**.

 Catherine Linton Heathcliff, daughter of **Catherine Earnshaw Linton**, is now engaged to **Hareton Earnshaw**, officially exhausting the **Emily Brontë's Brain-Numbingly Similar Name Generator** application.

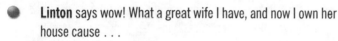 **Nelly** posted a news story.

Yorkshire Crier:
Mysterious, Sad Couple Seen Haunting Countryside

● **Lockwood** says there's not a ghost of a chance.

Travel Tipster Review of Wuthering Heights

"Very Disappointing, Local Ghost a Problem"

by Lockwood
December '01

Didn't have reservation and only stayed because of blizzard and dog attack. Staff consisted of rude young woman, guy who smelled of horse dung, servant who sicced said dogs on me, and so-called "master" of the house, who would be helpful if he didn't constantly look like he wants to kill everyone. The promised view from my room was blocked by annoying ghost that kept pretending to be a tree branch and moaning about being stuck on moors. Broken window and, of course, ghost led to chill in temperature, not healthy in house where dying due to consumption and all-around wimpiness seems rampant. When I complained to the "master," he berated me and forced me to walk around outside till dawn. Also, the sheets were kind of starchy.

Liked: Retro, gothic decor.

Disliked: Fearing my imminent death.

Would I recommend these accommodations to a friend? Only if by "friend" you mean someone I'd like to see put in a vice grip by a screeching lady-skeleton.

I recommend these accommodations for: necrophiliacs, Kate Bush.

I don't recommend these accommodations for: adults, children, honeymooners, older travelers, people with disabilities, tradesmen, farmhands, trick-or-treaters, gentry, ladies with a tendency to swoon, Haley Joel Osment, sleepwalkers, people who enjoy sanity.

The Brontë Sisters Play Scrabulific!

```
H E A T H
        A
    B U R N
        N
C A T A T O N I C
                L
                I
                F
                F
```

SMACK TALK!

Charlotte: "Cliff"? You're going to go for "cliff"? After starting with "heath"? Oh, that's creative.

Emily: I'm using the letters I have! And like the word "haunt" is so original. No one would ever expect that from the Brontës. Plus that second *F* is a double letter score.

Charlotte: I suppose next you're going to go for "love" or "swoon." Or "lust" and "hired help."

Emily: Oh, we're going there, are we? So what if Heathcliff has some attributes in common with the guy who grooms the horses. Write what you know, right? And I like a man with a little chip on his shoulder.

Charlotte: The other day he was threatening a bale of hay with a branding iron! And has he ever even talked to you, this guy you've based an iconic hero on?

Emily: Oh sure, and that guy you were a governess for, Mr. Cochester? He's SO going to sweep you up and marry you after never even looking at you ever. Good luck with that.

Charlotte: Really? Really? Let's talk about heroines. What IS up with Catherine? "Oh, we have the same soul, I'm going to haunt you forever, boooo, life is a prison, poor me!"

Emily: Right, and it makes so much MORE sense to collapse into a coma because of the color of a ROOM??

Charlotte: What? Can't hear you! I'm Catherine and I'm dying, dying, oh, you broke my heart, death, dying, woe woe woe.

Emily: Okay, I think I've got a real *F* word for you now. Triple word score.

Charlotte: Fine. I'm going to go post a picture of you from 1825.

Emily: FINE!

Charlotte: OKAY THEN!

Emily: Play again later, Currer?

Charlotte: Certainly, Ellis.

Anna Karenina

NEWS FEED

● **Leo Tolstoy** thinks every crazy family has its very own kind of crazy.

● **Prince** Stepan Arkadyich "Stiva" Oblons . . .

> **Admin**: Your name has exceeded the number of acceptable characters.

✎ **Stiva** has moved! At the request of his wife, **Dolly**, he now lives on his **Family's Sofa**.

✎ **Dolly** removed "French Governesses" from **Stiva's Interests**.

✉ **Stiva** sent a **Help Me Sister** request to **Anna Karenina**.

● **Anna** should be able to resolve all of this adultery mess.

> **Anna**: Solved!
>
> **Dolly**: Wow, you're good at this adultery mess.
>
> **Anna**: Yes, yes, I am.

🤝 **Anna** is now friends with **Vronsky**. **Anna** found **Vronsky** through the **People You May Know Because They're Courting Your Sister-in-Law's Sister** tool.

🎀 **Anna** sent **Vronsky** a **More-Than-Just-Friendly Smile** across a crowded train station.

● **A Watchman** has been hit by the train.

> **Stiva**: What a horrible way to die!
>
> **Anna**: Yes, yes, it is.

♟ **Kitty** is playing **Torn Between Two Suitors**. Help her choose!

—The **First Suitor** is **Vronsky**, a dashing military officer, one of the finest examples of the gilded youth of St. Petersburg.

—The **Second Suitor** is **Levin**, a landowner who might be socially awkward, fairly unattractive, and have a wild life in the country with his cattle and muzhiks, but he has a great big heart and really thinks about things, you know—a lot like Leo Tolstoy, actually—with really strong values and . . .

Kitty chose **Vronsky**! She turned down **Levin's** proposal and **Broke His Heart**.

Vronsky: Hello! What'd I miss?

● **Levin** isn't feeling very comfortable in this room anymore.

● **Levin** isn't feeling very comfortable in this room anymore.

Levin: Did I say that already?

Kitty's Eyes: Please forgive me. I'm just so happy.

Levin's Eyes: I hate everybody, especially myself.

✉ **Kitty**, **Levin**, **Vronsky**, and **Anna** are attending the **Big Russian Ball**.

● **Kitty** thinks Anna looks so nice tonight.

● **Kitty** is waiting for the mazurka.

● **Anna** is drunk on wine and the rapture she inspires.

● **Anna** is dancing circles around Kitty.

● **Anna** is dancing with Vronsky.

● **Kitty** doesn't need no stinking mazurka.

🎀 **Vronsky** sent **Kitty** a **Nearly Fatal, Heartbreak-Born Illness**.

● **Anna** thinks Vronsky should beg Kitty's forgiveness and stop looking at her that way.

Vronsky: But I love you with all of myself and can't think of you and myself separately anymore!

Anna: Never say those words to me! Let's be friends.

Anna's Eyes: The opposite of what I just said.

Anna's husband, Karenin: Hello! What'd I miss?

 Levin and **Kitty** are attending **The First Party We've Both Attended Since One of Us Broke the Other's Heart**.

 Levin challenged **Kitty** to a game of **Russian WordSpin: Now Way Harder Than English WordSpin**.

Levin's board: wyam:tcbdimnot? n? n?

Kitty's board: tlcgnoa and tyctatwh

Levin's board: lhntofaf!!! lhnsly! ☺

Kitty's board: Yes.

 Kitty and **Levin** are now married.

Karenin is appalled that Anna is having an affair!

Anna: Can I have a divorce?

Karenin: No.

Anna: Can I have a divorce?

Karenin: No.

Anna: I'm pregnant. Now can I have a divorce?

Karenin: No.

Anna: I had the baby, and I may be dying. Now can I have a divorce?

Karenin: Okay, though you could be disgraced. Why don't I leave it up to you?

> **Anna**: Oh, how big of you! Then I don't want a divorce.
>
> **Karenin**: Fine.
>
> **Anna**: I've been completely spurned by society. Now can I have a divorce?
>
> **Karenin**: No.
>
> **Anna**: And Vronsky's acting weird, and I've become addicted to sedatives.
>
> **Karenin**: No.
>
> **Anna**: Now?
>
> **Karenin**: Mmmm. Let me ask my French psychic. Yeah, still no.

Vronsky played **Russian Roulette** with a gun! Except it wasn't really roulette because he knew the chamber was loaded, and it was only Russian because he's Russian.

Vronsky, on top of being a bad horseman and fairly bad adulterer, is also apparently bad at shooting himself.

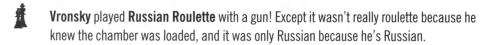 **Levin** upgraded to the **Family Plan**.

 **Levin** changed his **Religious Views** to "I Doubt Everything."

Levin changed his **Political Views** to "Conflicted."

Levin is now friends with **Anna Karenina**.

> **Levin**: She seems so NICE!
>
> **Kitty**: Really.

Levin talked Kitty down by about 3:00 in the morning.

Anna Karenina is now **Anna Paranoia**.

Anna will not give respect to Vronsky's mother.

Anna wrote on **Vronsky's Wall**.

"Sorry about the not respecting your mother. I love you! Come back!"

Anna wrote on **Vronsky's Wall**.

"Please? Please?"

Anna is not a fan of the train station. Or the people at the train station. Or of living.

Anna caught the train.

Levin found God.

> ✳ **John Milton** likes this.

Levin found out there's a lightning storm, and his wife and son are out there.

Levin is playing **Reality Check**! Finding his family safe and being hugely relieved by it means he wins the chance to have a **Good Life** lived among **Grown-ups**.

Levin is realizing he really loves his family.

> **Tolstoy**: No matter what kind of crazy they are.

MESSAGE FROM ADMIN:

Please note that *Anna Karenina*, though of course a wonderful novel, is more than eight hundred pages long. If we covered it all here, you would need a Spark Note of the news feed. Plus, do you really want to hear in great detail how Levin feels about agriculture right now? And city life versus country life in nineteenth-century Russia? And bureaucracies in St. Petersburg? And his conflicted thoughts on family life, akin to those of Kevin Bacon in *She's Having a Baby*? Tell you what. Go and put *She's Having a Baby* at the top of your DVD queue. Wait for it to arrive in the mail. Watch it, wonder a bit at the fact that Kevin Bacon in 1988 looks so similar to how he looks now while Alec Baldwin looks as if his current incarnation is a rascally great uncle to the one that was in that movie, and you will still get finished faster than we would trying to conquer this book.

The Scarlet Letter

NEWS FEED

Hester Prynne was tagged in the album **Puritan Adulteresses**.

Hester received **Punishment Flair**. She was sent an *A* to wear upon her chest and told she must stand before the town with her baby, **Pearl**.

Hester is not enjoying her flair.

A Mystery Man has joined the **Pointing and Staring Community**.

Hester thinks that Mystery Man looks awfully familiar. Like estranged-husband familiar.

> **Hester:** I thought he dwelt in AmsterdAm. Or wAs lost At seA.
>
> **Hester:** Is thAt Absolutely necessAry?
>
> **Hester:** DAmn.

Hester refuseth to post comments.

Dimmesdale received a **Make the Lady Tell Us Her Baby Daddy** request.

Dimmesdale wrote on **Hester's Wall**.

"I charge thee to speak out the name of thy fellow-sinner and fellow-sufferer! No? You sure? I guess she's not going to say it."

Hester wrote on **Dimmesdale's Wall**.

"No! My child has no earthly father! Certainly not anyone around here! No sir!"

Dimmesdale says see? Not anyone around here!

The Mystery Man updated his profile. He is now **Roger "The Leech" Chillingworth**.

? **Hester** has been **Imprisoned**! She can free herself by serving time and answering the following **Chillingworth Trivia Questions**:

> *Who is he, the man who hath wronged us both? Art thou not afraid of nightmares and hideous dreams? Why don't you like me?*

Hester got out of jail not quite free.

Chillingworth added the **Payback Time** application.

Hester and **Pearl** created their own network.

Hester became a fan of **Needlework**.

Pearl became a fan of **Outkast**.

Pearl is now friends with several imaginary people.

Dimmesdale isn't feeling so good.

Dimmesdale removed "women" from his **Interests**. Also "pleasure," "eating," and "air."

The Town sent **Dimmesdale** a **New House** next to a graveyard with a new roommate, **Mr. Chillingworth**!

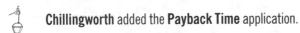

> **Dimmesdale**: Greeaat.

Chillingworth wonders why Dimmesdale gets so touchy when he brings up the topic of people who get diseased from hiding their horrific transgressions from God.

Chillingworth hazed **Dimmesdale**! He pulled the ol' **rip-open-the-guy's-shirt-while-he's-sleeping-to-see-if-he's-carved-an-*A*-in-his-flesh stunt.**

Chillingworth and **Dimmesdale** are no longer friends.

Dimmesdale is sermonizing about how evil he is.

Dimmesdale added "self-flagellation" to his **Interests**.

Hester and **Pearl** are attending **Dimmesdale's Pathetic Vigil on a Scaffold Meant for Public Flogging**.

 Dimmesdale knows this is weird, but that meteor really looks like the letter A.

> **Old Sexton**: Did you see that too? We think it stands for angel.
>
> **Dimmesdale**: Angel. Right.

 Hester sent a private message to **Dimmesdale**.

 Hester pulled a **Sexy Librarian**! She threw off the scarlet letter, let down her hair, and let loose her sex, youth, and beauty from the irrevocable past!

 Pearl posted an audio file of **her own piercing shrieks**.

 Hester restored her original profile picture.

 Dimmesdale invited **Hester** to attend a **European Vacation**.

 Hester sent **Free Love Feelings** to **Dimmesdale**.

 Dimmesdale earned a new **Lease on Life**! He is trying to resist using his points to disparage God in front of church elders, devastate religious old women, hang out with sailors, and teach swear words to children.

 Hester, **Pearl**, **Chillingworth**, **Dimmesdale**, and **All of Boston** are attending **Election Day**.

 The Narrator posted a **Video: Election Day Red Carpet Arrivals**.

> **Hester**: Why is everyone stAring?
>
> **Hester**: Still? ReAlly?

● **Hester** can't wait to get on that ship with Pearl and Dimmesdale and start a new life.

> **Sailor**: And with Chillingworth too? You know he's going.
>
> **Hester**: GreAt.

● **Dimmesdale** is preaching like his life depended on it.

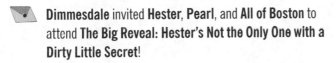 **Dimmesdale** invited **Hester**, **Pearl**, and **All of Boston** to attend **The Big Reveal: Hester's Not the Only One with a Dirty Little Secret**!

Dimmesdale removed "my shirt" from his **What I Am Wearing**.

> **Dimmesdale**: At lAst!
>
> **The Crowd**: Aha!
>
> **Chillingworth**: Ah !$#@!%#.
>
> **Hester**: FArewell.

Dimmesdale became a fan of the **Angels**.

Chillingworth was sent **Front-Row Seats to the Devils**.

● **Hester** returned to the place of her sorrow and her penitence.

 Hester received friend requests from **All of Boston**.

Hester and **Dimmesdale** received **Giant *As*** on their tombstones.

● **Witnesses** think Dimmesdale's death was a parable, telling us we're all sinners.

> **The reader**: Amen.

Video Transcript: Election Day Red Carpet Arrivals

Carson: You'd have to say that the ship's commander is making the biggest statement here. Look at all those ribbons! And that hat! Lace, *under* a gold chain, with a giant feather. It's amazing these Puritans don't just haul him off to the stocks right now.

Giuliana: Yeah, somehow he gets away with it. They *expect* him to go all out.

Carson: Speaking of extremes, is that Hester Prynne over thither?

Giuliana: Yes, Hester Prynne. Now this is her signature look.

Carson: Coarse gray cloth that makes it clear she'd like to blend in with the rocks on the ground. As always, the giant red symbol of her transgression against God, there on her bosom for all the world to see. That cap covering all of her hair—what color do you think it is?

Giuliana: Impossible to know, of course. But if I had to guess I'd say red, red like the heat of her loins when she took to her bed a man who was not her husband and damned herself for eternity. I do have to say, though, my favorite thing about her is that look on her face.

Carson: Yes! Frozen the way it is like a mask of some sort.

Giuliana: Like a piece of marble.

Carson: Like she's dead. A dead person.

Giuliana: Certainly dead inside. Now when we come back, we hope to talk to Minister Dimmesdale about his recent makeover. Has somebody finally found love?

3

Pip became a fan of Mean Girls.

The Coming of Age, or Not Network

Romeo and Juliet • The Adventures of Huckleberry Finn • To Kill a Mockingbird • Great Expectations and A Christmas Carol • The Catcher in the Rye • Little Women • Alice's Adventures in Wonderland

PROFILE

Basic Information

Network: Verona

Sex: Female

Relationship Status: It's complicated

Personal Information

Activities: Sighing, lounging, fanning myself, wishing a cute guy ☺☺ would come sweep me away, using my nurse as a mother figure because my own mother is always busy feuding with people (did you see that, MOTHER?)

Favorite Music: Anything on a lute, the Jonas Brothers

Favorite Movies: *West Side Story*, **HSM1,2&3!!!!!**

Favorite Quotations: "It is the east, and Juliet is the sun."—???

Wall

 Juliet posted an **Event**: **Party at My House!**

"capulets are throwing this to see if i have *sparks* with Paris. they want me to get MARRIED. Anyway, free wine."

● **Juliet OMG hooked up with random guy! Don't even know his NAME.**

> **Juliet:** Seriously, anyone know him? Darkhair hawt hawt blue doublet . . . if hes married I WILL DIE I MEAN IT.
>
> **Nurse:** I know who he is. Let's chat offline, shall we?

 Juliet updated her privacy settings. The **Capulet** network may no longer view her status updates, posts, photos, and friends.

Juliet is now friends with **Romeo**.

Juliet wrote a new **Note**: **WHY do you have to be ROMEO???????**

"IMHO Romeo should: Go against his dad Lose his STUUUUPID name OR Just say
♥♥♥♥♥ *me & I'll lose MY stupid name! What the $%@$ is in a name anyway? Get*
rid of your name ROMEO."

Romeo wrote

"SURE."

Juliet omigosh forgot you could see that ☺ i ♥ u so much!!!!!

> **Romeo**: I ♥♥♥♥♥♥♥♥ UUUUU so much.
>
> **Juliet**: i loveeeeeeeeeeeeeeeeeeeeeeeee uuuuuu romeeeeeeeeeeeeeeeeeeeeeeeeeeeeeeee
> eeeeeeeeeeeeeeeeeeo you are amazinggggggggggggggggg.

Juliet is loving her balcony right now.

> **Romeo**: Let's get married.
>
> **Juliet**: I'm thirteen.
>
> **Romeo**: I know a guy.
>
> **Juliet**: Wheeeee!!!!!!!!

 Juliet sent **1,000 Goodnights** to **Romeo**.

 Juliet accepted a **Sweet-Smelling Rose**, two **Crossed Stars**, a **Box of Chocolates**, a
Naughty Hug, three **Fish** for her **Ocean Reef**, a **Candy Heart ("I'm Yours")**, and the **1TRU**
♥ Flair from **Romeo**.

Juliet sent her **Nurse** a **Be My Messenger of Luv** request.

Juliet is wondering what's taking the Nurse so freaekin long!!!!!

> **Nurse**: I'm here. Just give me a minute.
>
> **Juliet**: One minute.
>
> **Nurse**: Just another minute.
>
> **Juliet**: One MORE minute.
>
> **Nurse**: What? Oh. Hey, where's your mom?

Juliet: Oh, COME ON.

Nurse: ROFL. Calm down. You can go meet Romeo at Friar Lawrence's. Jeez.

Juliet: FINALLY.

Nurse: No problem. You go and I'll just get a ladder and drag it back here for you—could be hard work, though that's nothing compared to the hard work of a husband if you know what I mean (LMAO).

Juliet is now married to **Romeo**.

Juliet will just go home & act like everything's normal (even if its so NOT normal im marrrrrrrrrrrrried ♥♥♥♥♥♥♥♥♥♥♥♥♥♥♥♥♥♥♥♥♥♥♥).

Romeo wrote

"im fortunes fool!!"

Juliet received a **message**.

Romeo is no longer listed in the Verona network.

Juliet wonders what the HEYELL is going on?????!!!??

Nurse: Woe! Death! Love and death and Romeo!

Juliet: Wait hes dead? ROMEO RU DEAD?

Juliet: Well if hes dead i might as well kill myself.

Juliet: Right now. OH GODDDD WHY ME IM DYINGGGG.

Nurse: What? No. Romeo killed your cousin Tybalt.

Juliet: ooooooooooooh is that all? * not killing self just yet *

Nurse: And Romeo's banished.

Juliet: OOOOOHHHHH SO MUCH WORSE THAN DEAD TYBALT ROMEO BANISHED NOOOOOO IM GOING TO DIE.

Nurse: Try and just hold yourself together for once? K? He's coming over.

Juliet sent **Romeo** a **Nightingale**.

Romeo: Nope. Its a lark unfortunately.

Juliet: Nightingale! Its totally nite right now and that lite is just a big meteor.

Romeo: No its day if i don't go ill be killlllled

Juliet: if u leave i WILL DIE

Romeo: i ♥♥♥♥♥♥♥♥♥♥♥ u soooooooo much I WILL DIE

Juliet: if u die ill die i ♥♥♥♥♥ u!!!!!!!!

Romeo: KISSSSSS me now or ill die xoxoxoxo

Juliet: i may nvr see u again oh go ill die ♥♥♥♥♥ xoxoxoxo

Romeo: loooooooooove u kiss u see u in death dethdd

Nurse: MOVE!

Juliet was invited to attend **Juliet and Paris's Wedding. Tomorrow**.

Juliet will never have Paris.

> **Juliet**: Hate him. HATE HATE DOUBLE HATE. Yuck ☹

Juliet received a **Magic Potion** from **Friar Lawrence**.

> **Friar Lawrence**: This will solve everything! Nothing could go wrong now.
>
> **William Shakespeare**: Right.

Juliet needs a drink.

> **Juliet**: idunno this could b really BAD but nothing else to do i ♥ him soooooo much ROMEO ROMEO ROMEO

This account has been temporarily deactivated.

This account is back online.

Juliet is AWAKE! That fake-death potion RAWKED!.

> **Juliet**: What'd I miss?

Juliet received a **Happy Dagger**.

This account has been permanently deactivated.

Inbox

Romeo Montague

UNREAD

Friar L	**RE: The plan**
	Hope you get this message—I think the last one didn't go through . . .
Juliet	**RE: tonight**
	Hi husband! Husband! OMG luv it. Tho u know I can't take your name . . .
Benvolio	**RE: Rosaline**
	IMHO you should find a rebound grl. Let's check out this party tonight . . .
Mercutio	**RE: pricking**
	Dude! Blow off Rosaline (heh). U just need somewhere to put your . . .
Rosaline	**RE: tonight**
	Luv u so much Rome. Tru luv! They'll write books about us we . . .

From Friar L

Today at 6:15 pm

Romeo—

Hope you get this message—I think the last one didn't go through. Some sort of quarantine? Just wanted to let you know, I've given a special potion to Juliet to solve all this craziness. It'll make her look dead— quite, quite dead — but she won't be dead. I repeat, NOT dead. Looking dead. But NOT. And, thanks to this message, you'll be there, all ready for her to wake up and start your lives together. Long, wonderful, love-filled lives, even though all week the signs have been pointing to short, unhappy, very ended-too-soon lives. But that's clearly wrong because here I am writing you this note, which you'll see there in Mantua and then you'll come to Verona and be there when she wakes up. Because she's NOT dead. As I mentioned.

If for some reason you heard she was dead and you didn't get this note, knowing you, you'd do something impulsive! But I'm sure it'll all work out. And have fun, kids. You crazy, crazy kids.

All best.

Friar Lawrence

The Adventures of Huckleberry Finn

NEWS FEED

- **Huckleberry Finn** took a vacation and enjoyed some relaxation.

- **Huck** switched his **Language** preferences to **English (Mark Twain)**.

- **Huck** lit out and was free and satisfied.

- **Huck** was invited to rejoin the **St. Petersburg, Not the One in Russia** network.

- **Widow Douglas** sent **Huck** some **New Clothes**, some **Learnin' About Moses**, and a **Talking To**.

- **Huck** is feelin' tired and lonesome.

- **Miss Watson** told Huck he'll be a-going to the bad place if he don't behave.

- **Huck** would gladly go anywhere's not involving Miss Watson.

- **Tom Sawyer** added "Don Quixote, The Count of Monte Cristo, and other books 'bout adventures and robbin' and murderin' and ransomin' people" to his **Favorite Books**.

- **Tom** would like to try robbin' and murderin' and ransomin' people.

- **Huck's** just worried that Pap will come back. Oh $?@#$%!

- **Pap** commented on **Huck's** profile picture.

"Well, look at YOU. Don't you give me none o' your lip. I'll take you down a peg. You think you're better'n your father? All hifalut'n and a-swelling yourself up. I'll learn you to put on airs. I'll tan your hide. Now give me your money."

? **Pap** scored 100 percent on the **Are You an After-school Special Abusive Dad?** quiz.

● **Pap** went a-blowing and cussing and whooping and carrying on all over town.

📜 **Huck** has been **Kidnapped** by **Pap** to a ramshackle cabin! He used **Idiocy** and **The Fact I'm Bigger'n You** trick.

♟ **Huck** played **Dead**.

● **Mark Twain** says reports of Huck's death are greatly exaggerated.

● **Huck** hightailed it to Jackson Island.

● **Jim** hightailed it to Jackson Island.

🍬 **Huck** is now friends with **Jim**.

● **Huck** is itchin' to get a-stirring up somehow.

♟ **Jim** suggested an information gathering game for Huck: **Dress Up Like a Girl and Go to Town**.

? **Huck** took the quiz **What Girl Are You?** with the result "Sarah Williams, or was it Mary Williams? Dern it. I guess maybe I'm George Peters."

● **Huck** and **Jim** now need to flee quick as possible.

⚱ **Jim** and **Huck** added the **Build Your Own Raft** application.

● **Jim** is passing the great lights of St. Louis with Huck.

Huck and **Jim** sent each other **Shipwreck Loot**.

Huck laid off all the afternoon with Jim, talking and having a general good time.

Huck says it feels mighty free and easy and comfortable on a raft.

> **Jim:** Well, easy and comfortable anyway.

 Huck and **Jim** requested an **Ohio River: Exit Here for Freedom** notice and instead received a **Mississippi Blinding Fog**.

 Huck played a **Dirty Trick** on **Jim**! He won 40 points in feelin' mean and ashamed and a-wishing he could take it back.

 Huck added the **Moral Quandary** application.

 Huck and **Jim** are now friends with **The Duke** and **Dauphin** through the **People You're Stuck with Because They're on Your Raft** tool.

 The Dauphin joined the group **Kings of France Who Don't Speak French**.

 The Duke joined the group **Dukes Who Hawk Tartar-Takin'-Off Remedies**.

**Huck** posted a **Note**.

> *Stuff White People on the River Seem to Like: angry mobs, blood feuds, drunken brawls, swindling folks, running rapscallions out of town on a rail, the circus.*

 The Duke and **Dauphin** added the **Bogus Scams** application, the **Inciting Bloodthirsty Uprisings** application, the **Worst-Ever Fake British Accents** tool, the **Hoodwink a Whole Town** game, the **Rob a Dead Man** application, and **You Should Be Ashamed of Yourselves** awards.

Huck added "Learning people can really suck sometimes" to his **Education Info**.

 Jim has been **Kidnapped** to the **Phelps Farm**!

Huck is writing a letter to tell Miss Watson where Jim is.

Huck is remembering that Jim voted Huck his Best Friend in All the World.

- Huck is remembering all the great times they had.

- Huck is ripping up the letter.

- Huck don't care no more if he's a-going to the bad place.

- Sally Phelps is waiting for her nephew Tom Sawyer to visit.

- Huck changed his profile. He is now **Tom Sawyer**.

- Tom Sawyer came to town.

- Tom changed his profile. He is now **Sid Sawyer**.

- Huck shared a **Free Jim Plan** with **Tom**.

- Tom became a fan of **Breaking and Entering, But Only in a Romantic, Convoluted Way Like Is the Custom in Europe by the Best Authorities in Writin' Novels**.

- Tom sent **Jim** a **Freedom-Making Variety Pack** with candleholders, bedsheets, case knives, tin plates, and fox fire.

- Tom has leveled up in **Overcomplicating Pursuits**. He earned the chance to **Almost Get Them All Killed** and a **Bullet in His Log**.

- Jim sent **A Doctor** a **Map**: Where to go to get Tom help even if it risks my freedom.

- Tom tried the new game **Honesty**.

- Tom explained Jim was free all along.

- Huck has had it with just about all of these folks. (Except Jim.)

- Huck will deactivate his account, 'cause he reckons there's nothing else worth writing 'bout and he's not stickin' around to have Aunt Sally try to sivilize him.

- Huck has already added "Bein' sivilized" to his **Places I've Been**.

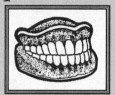

To Kill a Mockingbird
NOTE

🔖 Five Random Things About Boo Radley

by Scout Finch

Rules: If somebody goes and tags you, you've got to write lots and lots of things about yourself. I can't think of any things for myself, so I might as well do them on Boo Radley seein' as he's all we talk about. Also, I only did five.

1. Boo Radley breathes on azaleas and makes them freeze.

2. Boo Radley mutilates chickens and household pets.

3. Boo Radley commits stealthy small crimes around Maycomb.

4. Boo Radley stabbed his dad in the leg with some scissors.

5. Boo Radley is about six-and-a-half feet tall; dines on raw squirrels and cats; has a long jagged scar, popped eyes, and yellow, rotten teeth; and drools most of the time.

COMMENT

Atticus: Now, Scout, this isn't very kind. Remember what I told you? That you'll never understand a person until you climb into his skin and walk around in it?

Calpurnia: Yes, indeed. You need to show some respect to your neighbors.

Scout: But I heard it. It's all true!

Atticus: Scout.

Calpurnia: Scout.

Jem: Yeah, Scout, what's your problem?

Scout: You HUSH, Jem. You told me that stuff in the first place!

〜 Five OTHER Random Things About Boo Radley

by Scout Finch

1. Boo Radley doesn't have the ability to sneeze.

2. Boo Radley played Nathan Detroit in the original *Guys and Dolls*.

3. Boo Radley wrote the Declaration of Independence.

4. Boo Radley is Deputy Regional Manager, Southeast Division.

5. Boo Radley invented the airplane.

COMMENT

Atticus: Miss Jean Louise Finch, these are all completely imaginary.

Scout: Aw, but they're not mean anymore! I just liked writin' 'em.

Atticus: Well, I think you should try again. In fact, why don't you write some things about yourself?

Scout: Yes, sir.

Jem: Yeah, Scout, try and do it right this time, why don't ya?

Scout: Hush your mouth, Jem! Shoot.

〜 Five Dumb Things About Me, Scout Finch

by Scout Finch

1. I'm learning the Dewey Decimal System in school.

2. I don't much like school.

3. I sometimes beat up stupid boys.

4. I can't think up anything to write about myself.

5. I think Boo Radley once talked a mountain lion outta eatin' him up.

Scout's Playlist

"Small Town"
"Sweet Home Alabama"
"I Fought the Law"
"Papa Don't Preach"
"My Heart Belongs to Daddy"
"Just a Girl"
"My Boo"

COMMENT

> **Atticus**: Okay, Scout. Maybe your intention to think about people other than yourself was a good one. You can write five more things about Boo Radley, but then that's the end of this exercise, you hear?
>
> **Jem**: You hear, Scout?
>
> **Scout**: Why don't you take a look at #3, Jem.

Five Things About Boo Radley

by Scout Finch

1. Boo Radley mended Jem's pants (which he caught on a fence while running from the Radley house).

2. Boo Radley makes tiny figurines of people out of soap (which at first I thought was hoodoo, but it's really kinda nice).

3. Boo Radley secretly gave me and Jem some gum (which was pretty fresh and wasn't poisoned like I thought).

4. Boo Radley put a blanket round my shoulders when Miss Maudie's house was on fire (and it was the coldest winter since 1885!).

5. Boo Radley I think maybe saved my life. And Jem's too.

COMMENT

> **Atticus**: Now, isn't that much better?
>
> **Calpurnia**: Don't you feel more grown-up, Scout?
>
> **Jem**: I declare you're getting more like a girl every day!
>
> **Scout**: Thank you . . .
>
> **Scout**: Aw, that was an insult, wasn't it! But I got you back cause I tagged you in this note, Jem. I tagged you! You're it.

Great Expectations
NEWS FEED

● **Pip** is visiting his parents in the cemetery.

 Pip was recruited to play **Jailbreak**! He just got startled by a **Terrifying Convict**!

> **Charles Dickens**: He's a fearful man, all in coarse gray, with a great iron on his leg. A man with no hat and with broken shoes.
>
> **Pip**: Agh!
>
> **Charles Dickens**: A man who had been soaked in water, smothered in mud, lamed by stones, cut by flints.
>
> **Pip**: Scary!
>
> **Charles Dickens**: A man stung by nettles and torn by briars. A man who limped and shivered and glared and growled.
>
> **Convict**: Get me some wittles, or your heart and liver shall be tore out, roasted, and ate!
>
> **Pip**: !!

● **Charles Dickens** is frightening the bejeezus out of children everywhere.

 Pip commented on his own photo, **My "Family."**

> *"My brother-in-law Joe is a sort of Hercules in strength, and also in weakness. My sister, Mrs. Joe, looks like she washes herself with a nutmeg-grater."*

> **Mrs. Joe**: Hah! Who brought you up by hand?
>
> **Pip**: You did.
>
> **Mrs. Joe**: I'd never do it again! You great stuck pig!

● **Mrs. Joe** is diving at Pip, fishing him up by the hair, and dousing him with tar-water.

> **Joe**: Well, I . . .

 Mrs. Joe is taking Joe by the whiskers and knocking his head against the wall.

 Pip and **Joe** joined the group **Males Who Should Keep Their Hair and Whiskers as Short as Possible**.

 Pip is playing **Jailbreak Level 2: Aiding and Abetting**! He gave the **Convict Bread**, **Cheese**, **Mincemeat**, **Brandy**, a **Metal File**, and a **Beautiful Pork Pie**. If he doesn't get caught, he'll move to the next level and win **Not Being Pummeled by Mrs. Joe**.

 Pip is so scared he'd feel pain in his liver if he knew where it was.

 Pip is having Christmas dinner with a bunch of Dickensian characters.

 A Soldier posted a news item.

> *Convicts on the loose! Broken handcuffs and pork pie crumbs found at the scene.*

 Pip and **Joe** were invited to play **Manly Criminal Chase** in the **Misty Marshes**.

 The Terrifying Convicts lost this round of **Jailbreak**. They'll be sent back to the prison ship, bound to haunt Pip's dreams forevermore.

Miss Havisham sent **Pip** a **Friend Demand**.

Pip commented on his own photo, **My Playdate**.

> *"So I think this is a dressing room? There seemed to be a once-white, now-yellow theme. All the clocks were stopped at twenty to nine. It's not the best image due to the lack of any ounce of daylight and the skeleton lady swatting at me."*

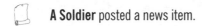 **Miss Havisham** long ago became a fan of **The Grudge**.

Miss Havisham has posted a vintage wedding gown. Also, vintage wedding cake, vintage dust, vintage odor, vintage crazy.

> **Miss Havisham**: I am tired. I want diversion. Play!
>
> **Estella**: Don't loiter, boy. He calls the knaves jacks, this boy. What coarse hands and thick boots, this boy.

● **Estella** bossed Pip around and made him feel bad about himself, his family, and his class.

> **Estella**: I'm going to make you cry, boy.

Pip became a fan of **Mean Girls**.

● **Pip** is walking Miss Havisham in circles while she yells at people.

Miss Havisham sent **Estella** a secret request: **BREAK HIS HEART**.

● **Pip** is just enjoying not being bashed against the wall for a little while.

Mrs. Joe and **Orlick** are now **Sworn Enemies**.

Mrs. Joe received a **Thump on the Head with Something Heavy** from a mystery person!

● **Mrs. Joe** won't be bashing anyone from now on.

Pip received **One Giant Status Update**.

Pip received a **Brand New Life** from a **Secret Benefactor**.

Pip added **Jaggers** as his new **Creepy Guardian**.

Pip joined the **London** network.

Pip added 16 new profile pictures.

Pip added "I have many, actually, let me tell you about them" to his **Political Views**.

Pip joined the group **I Secretly Want to Punch Anyone Inferior to Me in the Back of the Head**.

Pip added "Being idle, idling, counting my money, doing nothing, learning how to use silverware, staying in hotels in my own hometown because my family is beneath me, laughing at common people, and interior design" to his **Interests**.

- **Pip** is embarrassed to be around Joe.

- **Pip** is now friends with **Herbert Pocket**, **Matthew Pocket**, and **Mr. Wemmick**.

- **Pip** can't talk now, he's busy de-friending people.

- **Pip** thinks it's great Miss Havisham has been his secret benefactor all these years.

- **Pip** is being visited by a strange-looking gentleman who looks awfully familiar.

> **Charles Dickens**: He was substantially dressed, but roughly, like a voyager by sea.
>
> **Pip**: Agh!
>
> **Charles Dickens**: He had long iron-gray hair. He was a muscular man, browned and hardened by weather.
>
> **Pip**: Okay, okay.

- **Pip** now sees the **Mystery Gentleman** in his **Some People You May Know**. They're both friends with **Jaggers** and **Wemmick**.

> **Pip**: Right, but that couldn't mean . . .
>
> **Magwitch the Ex-Convict**: I'm your benefactor, Pip! I'm like your second father!

- **Pip** will have to go change everything in his profile now, apparently.

- **Pip** is realizing he was just a Boy Toy for Estella and Miss Havisham.

- **Estella** is now married to **Bentley Drummle**.

- **Pip** thinks maybe he shouldn't have trusted an old shriveled woman who's been wearing a wedding dress for three or four decades.

- **Miss Havisham** will just pick up that thing she dropped really close to the fireplace.

- **Miss Havisham** joined the group **Maidens Who Are Not Inflammable**.

Pip is playing **Converging Plot Points**! **Magwitch's** old fellow convict, **Compeyson**, is the guy who left **Miss Havisham** at the altar. **Molly**, the familiar-looking servant at **Mr. Jaggers'** house, is **Estella's** mother, making **Magwitch Estella's** father!

> **Pip**: What a coincidence!
>
> **Charles Dickens**: Not really!

And **Orlick**, who despises **Pip**, just seems to have drifted out of the story for no reason.

 Pip is attending a **Meeting on the Marshes Where Bad Things Always Happen**.

> **Charles Dickens**: Hmm.

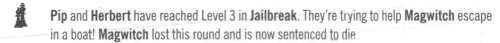 **Orlick** tried to **choke Pip with a noose**! **Use a hammer to kill with, cook in a blacksmith's kiln, throw a mince pie at**, or **just sit there and feel sorry for yourself**.

● **Pip** is blanking on this part while some other men save his life.

 Pip and **Herbert** have reached Level 3 in **Jailbreak**. They're trying to help **Magwitch** escape in a boat! **Magwitch** lost this round and is now sentenced to die.

● **Pip** is really sorry about that.

● **Pip** is now sorry about a lot of things, actually.

 Pip's account has been infiltrated by a virus.

● **Pip** lost all of his money and might have to go to debtor's prison.

● **Pip** could swear all the people from his past are now visiting him.

> **Pip**: Is it Joe?
>
> **Joe**: It air, old chap, dear old Pip. I meantersay what larks!

〇 **Pip** and **Joe** are now friends. Top Friends. Ever Friends.

 Pip added "An Honest, Modest Job" to his **Work Info**.

● **Pip** ran into Estella on the street in London. Her life turned out crappy and maybe now she has some inkling of how Pip felt when she was cruel to him.

> **Charles Dickens**: Wait. Kind of bleak, yeah?

● **Pip** found Estella in the ruins of Miss Havisham's house. He took her hand and doesn't think he'll ever not see her again.

> **Charles Dickens**: It could happen.

Miss Havisham

PROFILE

Basic Information

Networks: Satis House

Relationship Status: HAHAHAHAHAHAHAHAHAHAHA!

Personal Information

Favorite Music: "Crazy," "Crazy Train," "Crazy"

Favorite TV Shows: *Whose Wedding Is It Anyway?*, *The Bachelor*, *A Wedding Story*, *Millionaire Matchmaker*, *Platinum Weddings*, *BRIDEZILLLLLLLLLLLLLLAS*

Favorite Movies: *Kill Bill*

Wall

 Miss Havisham is HERE—of course, I'm HERE, where else would I be but HERE?????
I will never leave!

 Miss Havisham WHAT IF YOU PUT ON A WEDDING DRESS AND NO ONE CAME?

 Miss Havisham I'M SHOUTING BECAUSE MY EARS ARE FILLED WITH SPIDERS!

 Miss Havisham can stop time! BREAKTHEIRHEARTS!

 Miss Havisham I only have one shoe on!!!!!!!!!!!!!!!!!!!!!

A Christmas Carol

NEWS FEED

Scrooge would like you to stop looking at his profile.

Scrooge will not accept your friend request.

Scrooge sent a request to have you take your **Glowing Christmas Tree**, **X-mas Gifts!**, **Holiday Ornaments**, **Friendly Snowballs**, and **Secret Santas** and **Humbug** them **Up the Humbug** all the way back to **Humbug Town**.

Scrooge is seeing dead people.

Scrooge is regretting ever friending Jacob Marley.

Marley will send **Scrooge** three **Spirits** and possible **Redemption**.

Scrooge is still just thinking he ate a bad potato.

The Ghost of Christmas Past shared a **Link** with **Scrooge**: **Old Home Movies**.

The Ghost of Christmas Present sent **Scrooge** a **Reality Check**.

The Ghost of Christmas Yet to Come sent **Scrooge** a **Potential Horrible Death Scene**.

Scrooge would like to change the settings in his View.

Scrooge sent **Bob Cratchit** a **Prize-Winning Turkey**.

Scrooge is now friends with **Fred and his wife**.

Scrooge sent a **Kind Smile** to **Everybody**, who somehow forgot his lifetime of bad behavior.

Tiny Tim was sent a **New Lease on Life**.

Tiny Tim sent a **Blessing** request to **God**, for everyone.

Holden Caulfield would like to apologize in advance for anything he's about to say here, if you really want to know the truth.

> ✴ **Boo-Boo Glass** and 6 others like this.

Holden Caulfield is waiting.

Holden Caulfield is waiting.

Holden Caulfield is still waiting.

Holden Caulfield is getting drunk in a cheap hotel.

> **Boo-Boo Glass**: Noooooo!
>
> **Buddy Glass**: You were doing so well!
>
> **Holden Caulfield**: Well, nothing was happening! It's goddam humiliating.
>
> **Phoebe Caulfield**: Oh, Holden, it was only twenty minutes! Not everybody has time to watch status updates all day long. Maybe Jane didn't see it yet.
>
> **Huck Finn**: I reckon' maybe Jane goes to school like some people do.
>
> **Holden Caulfield**: Thing is, Jane isn't my "friend" yet. I never felt like asking her.
>
> **Buddy Glass**: What??
>
> **Boo-Boo Glass**: You're not serious.
>
> **Jo March**: What was the point to all this then?
>
> **Scout Finch**: I don't understand this game anyway.

Holden Caulfield is in a cab that smells like someone just tossed his cookies in it.

> **Buddy Glass**: Okay, I give up. I've got to go on this radio show.
>
> **Boo-Boo Glass**: Me too.
>
> **Huck Finn**: Gotta get back to the raft.
>
> **Jo March**: I think I need to go sing or quilt or something.
>
> **Pip**: I have to go get ordered around by a little girl.

> **Scout Finch**: I have to go order around some little boys.
>
> **Phoebe Caulfield**: Holden, I have to go to bed. But I'll help you tomorrow.
>
> **Holden Caulfield**: Old Phoebe, she kills me. She really does.

Holden Caulfield shouldn't have told everybody everything, cause if you do you start . . .

Holden Caulfield received a friend request.

Holden Caulfield is now friends with **Jane Gallagher**.

Holden Caulfield is feeling so damn happy all of a sudden.

> **Holden Caulfield**: I'm not kidding.
>
> **Holden Caulfield**: I'm happy.
>
> **Holden Caulfield**: I really am.
>
> **Boo-Boo Glass**: All right!
>
> **Phoebe Caulfield**: Yay, Holden!
>
> **Jo March**: How nice.
>
> **Buddy Glass**: Now just don't screw it up.

Holden Caulfield played a round of **Checkers**.

Holden Caulfield did not go to a bar, hang out with crumby girls, say something mortifying, break into anyplace, or get kicked out of anywhere today.

> **Buddy Glass**: Okaaaay.
>
> **Boo-Boo Glass**: I guess it's not terrible.

Holden Caulfield just still wants to know about those ducks in the lagoon in Central Park, that little lake, and where they go, the ducks, when it gets all frozen over.

> **Boo-Boo Glass**: All right, all right. I think this is good for now.
>
> **Jo March**: It's still weird, but at least you're being yourself.

Buddy Glass: You're definitely on your way, Holden. You don't need us anymore.

Pip: Cheers!

Boo-Boo Glass: Ta-ta.

Jo March: Good-bye.

Scout Finch: See ya.

Holden Caulfield: But really, where do they go? The ducks? Does anybody know? In the winter? When the lagoon is frozen?

Holden Caulfield: Aw, you bunch of phonies. I don't even know why I log in sometimes. You bastards.

Holden Caulfield: Except Phoebe, she kills me. I swear to God.

Phoebe Caulfield: I'm still here.

Holden Caulfield: Okay.

Little Women

NEWS FEED

- **Jo March** is not looking forward to Christmas.

    > **Meg**: It's so dreadful to be poor!
    >
    > **Amy**: It's not fair other girls get pretty things and we don't!
    >
    > **Beth**: We've got our family, and that's all I need to be happy.

- **Jo** thinks they could all use a little fun.

    > **Louisa May Alcott**: And then Meg says something about having to be responsible, and Jo says something tomboyish . . .
    >
    > **And Amy**: (Something about her looks.)
    >
    > **And Beth**: (Something sweet and gentle, making them all feel guilty.)
    >
    > **Meg**: Oh, how happy we'd be if we weren't unhappy!

- **Mr. March** wrote on **Marmee's Wall**.

    > *"Here at the Civil War, things aren't that bad! I've just eaten a hunk of something cooked on a campfire, and the men singing the 'Battle Hymn of the Republic' over and over really drown out the shouts of ~~pain horror abject terror~~ comradery! Please tell the children I am ever so proud of my little women. And I'm sorry this letter couldn't be longer, but we need the paper to make boots for some of the men."*

- **Marmee** would like the girls to think of what we've learned from *The Pilgrim's Progress*, and remember that goodness and happiness are the guides that lead us through trouble and mistakes down the road to the Celestial City.

    > **Beth**: Now let's all sing a round of "Crinkle, crinkle, 'ittle 'tar"!

● **Louisa May Alcott** is so tired of this moral pap.

✎ **Louisa** posted a **Note**.

> *Really, I know I wrote this, and okay, it might be slightly autobiographical (I'm the tomboyish second daughter of four girls who likes to write, my dad was terrible with money, and my sister Elizabeth SPOILER ALERT died of scarlet fever). But had I known it was going to be such a megahit that I'd have to write all these sequels—Little Men? Jo's Boys?—I'm not sure I'd have bothered with these people. I know Thoreau and Emerson and Hawthorne! (Or at least they live by me.) I should be taken more seriously! Plus, a male character named Laurie Laurence? What was I thinking?*

● **Louisa** will just speed things up here.

● **Jo** is doing some awkward and unladylike things.

● **Jo** and all of the Marches are blowing off housework and spoiling their dinner, but it's HILARIOUS.

● **Jo** got a haircut (very dramatic)

 Beth was sent **Scarlet Fever** (I warned you).

 Amy and **Laurie** are now married.

● **Amy** became much sweeter, deeper, and more tender.

 Jo (due to the quite inane response of my readers because I really would have liked her to stay a strong, literary, independent woman) and her **Professor** are now married.

● **Jo** doesn't think she should ever call herself 'Unlucky Jo' again because all of her dreams have come true!

> **Louisa**: You see? See what I'm dealing with?
>
> **Marmee**: Dear Jo, I know your harvest will be a good one.
>
> **Jo**: (Something funny and dear about sowing and reaping.)

Neo: Ah, the White Rabbit.

Charlie Pace: Are you referring to the Dharma logo on the Looking Glass station as seen in the last episode of Season 3 of *Lost*?

Jack Shepherd: Maybe she means when I was following the ghost of my father around the island in Season 1, Episode 5, which is named, duh, "White Rabbit."

Kate Austen: She could mean ANY episode of *Lost*! We're one giant rabbit hole out here!

Sawyer: Chill, Freckles, and ignore Dr. Do-Right over there. You want a bunny? I'll get you a bunny.

Alice: What I mean is, this rabbit came running by me in a plaid waistcoat and took out a pocket watch, said he was late, then jumped down a hole, so I followed. Oh, how I fell! How brave they'll think me at home when I tell them!

Dorothy Gale: Not necessarily.

Harry Potter: Word.

 Alice wishes she could stop changing so much.

Gregor Samsa and **Dr. Jekyll** like this.

Margaret: Are you there God? It's me, Margaret. I'm worried Alice is going through puberty and soon she'll have to wear deodorant. Please don't let her menstroo-ate before me. Thank you.

Alice: No, you see, as the hookah-smoking Caterpillar told me, if you eat from one side of the mushroom, you get larger . . .

Grace Slick: And your mind is *moooo*ving slow.

Alice: Well. And from the other side, you get smaller. I just want to be my right size.

Margaret: Are you there, God? I know Alice got IT and I'm the only one who isn't going to get IT. I know it, God. And I still have nothing to put in my bra. Please help me grow, God. You know where. Thank you.

● **Alice** does wish I didn't have to keep changing! I would cry, but I did that before and almost drowned myself in my poor tears. Along with several woodland creatures.

> **Peter Pan**: You don't have to change, Alice. Never grow up!
>
> **Lewis Carroll**: Here, here!
>
> **Hans Christian Andersen**: So true!
>
> **Humbert Humbert**: Yes, yes!
>
> **Holden Caulfield**: This place is lousy with perverts.

● **The White Rabbit** can't believe how late it's getting. Oh, my dear paws.

● **The Mad Hatter** reserved a teatime.

● **Alice** thinks everyone has such a queer way of talking. Which way do I go?

> **Cheshire Cat**: Depends where you want to get to.
>
> **March Hare**: Just say what you mean.
>
> **Alice**: I do! I mean, I mean what I say, you see.
>
> **Caterpillar**: I don't see.
>
> **Tweedledum**: I know what you think, but it isn't so.
>
> **Tweedledee**: Contrariwise, if it was so, it might be.
>
> **Harry Caray**: It might be, it could be, it is!
>
> **Lewis Carroll**: All mimsy were the borogoves, and the mome raths outgrabe.
>
> **James Joyce**: Alicious, twinstreams twinestraines, through alluring glass or alas in jumboland?

? **Alice** took the quiz **What Drink Are You?** with the result "Shirley Temple."

● **The Mad Hatter** wonders what drink he would be if they had any drinks left at this tea party that never ends.

> **Grace Slick**: Go ask Alice. I think she'll know!
>
> **Alice**: No, I really don't. I'm still trying to figure out how to use a flamingo for a croquet mallet.
>
> **The Queen**: Off with her head!
>
> **Alice**: Wonderland can be so very unpleasant.

 Alice received a **Summons**! Six more trials and she'll move up a level to **Badgered Witness**.

> **The King**: Persons more than a mile high should leave the court!
>
> **Alice**: I am not a mile high!
>
> **The Queen**: More like two miles.
>
> **Hunter S. Thompson**: Right on.
>
> **Grace Slick**: *Remember* what the dormouse said!
>
> **Alice**: Treacle? The dormouse kept talking about treacle.
>
> **Humbert Humbert**: I've got some treacle, my precocious pet.
>
> **White Rabbit**: Oh, my ears and whiskers.

● **Alice** figured out the size thing, I **think**. I think. Oh.

> **Lewis Carroll**: It's just a metaphor, you see, for the confusion that comes with growing older.
>
> **Margaret**: Are you there, God? Are you? ARE YOU?
>
> **James Joyce**: Alis, alas, she broke the glass! Liddell lokker through the leafery.
>
> **Alice**: won od ot tahw rednow od I, em raeD

Lewis Carroll: You see, she's so confused she's commenting backwards, as if in a Looking Glass!

Alice: ddo yrev s'ti siht ekil t'nod yllaer I

Alice: pots ot ti tnaw tsuj, suoiruc regnol on m'I

Alice: Oh this sucks. I'm just going to start a blog.

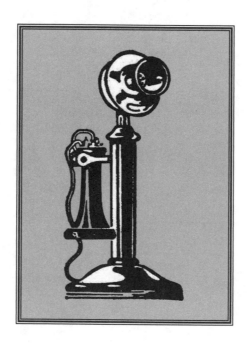

4

Ishmael says call me.

The Man versus Society Network

Shakespeare's Histories • Moby-Dick • Gulliver's Travels • A Farewell to Arms •
Ernest Hemingway • 1984 and Brave New World • Gone with the Wind •
Lord of the Flies • Don Quixote

Shakespeare's Histories

NEImages FEED

William Shakespeare is reimagining the reigns of the houses of Lancaster and York and, before them, the reign of the Plantagenet line that ended with Richard II.

> **Richard II**: What the hell?

Richard II sent a **Permission to Duel** to **Thomas Mowbray** and **My Annoying Cousin Henry**.

> **Richard II**: What do I care if you two poke each other to death? Or super-poke!!

Richard II has canceled the duel and sent **Banishments** to **Thomas** and **Henry**.

> **Richard II**: I don't care how much the "people" like you, Henry. What does that have to do with me? I'm the king you know.

Richard II is the KING. And just because I've racked up a few bills and listened too much to bad advisors, when did that ever affect a political leader?

> **Richard II**: Right, Shakespeare, I'm sure you have opinions on that too.

Richard II thinks John of Gaunt is just soooo poetic on his deathbed.

 Richard II added "this scepter'd isle, this earth of majesty . . . this blessed plot, this earth, this realm, this England!" to his **Favorite Quotations**.

> **Richard II**: It's not bad, actually.

 John of Gaunt sent **Richard** an **Ominous Curse**.

> **Richard II**: Ooooooh, a curse as you're dying? In a Shakespeare play? I'm really scared. Spooky!

> **Richard II**: Shut UP, William.

● **Richard II** is not so happy to hear Henry is building an army to overthrow me. But I've still got all my loyal supporters. No?

> **Richard II**: Okay, who removed "King of England" from my **Work Info**?

● **Richard II** is hiding in a castle.

> **Richard II**: Wait, no. Not hiding! Waiting. For my return! And hey, Henry, how about I give you a curse of your own!

 Richard II became a fan of **There Will Be Blood**.

> **Richard II**: Yeah, Henry will see how hard being king is.
>
> **Richard II**: Who the hell are you?

This account now belongs to Henry IV.

● **Henry IV** totally did not mean to have Richard killed! That's so funny you think that. But now that he's dead, it kind of eases the mind, you know?

> **Henry IV**: But, you know, who doesn't ease my mind? My son, Harry.

● **Henry IV** wonders if maybe his son, the heir to the throne, now hanging out with a giant, flatulent idiot and his moronic minions, was switched at birth.

 Henry IV received a **Poo Fart** from **Falstaff**.

> **Henry IV**: You see what I'm dealing with?

● **Henry IV** thinks maybe he should've sent a thank-you to Hotspur and his family for ridding the kingdom of Richard. Not that I had anything to do with that.

> **Henry IV**: I'm pretty sure Hotspur knows I appreciated it.

 Hotspur sent **Henry IV** an **Attempted Coup**.

 Harry accepted a **Help Me Save Our Kingdom** request from **Henry IV**.

> **Henry IV**: But you just HAD to bring Falstaff with you, didn't you.

● **Henry IV** is saved! My son saved my life! Maybe there's hope for that kid yet!

> **Henry IV**: Wait, where'd he go?

● **Henry IV** isn't feeling that well.

> **Henry IV**: It's not easy being king. You get insomnia and feel bad about the wars and my son who will soon be Henry V, I guess. And the killing Richard. I mean. Oh, I'm tired.

This account now belongs to Henry V.

▥ **Henry V** changed his profile picture.

> **Henry V**: Does this crown look all right? It's kind of uncomfortable.

🍬 **Falstaff** is someone **Henry V** might know.

> **Henry V**: Nope. Don't know the guy.

🎀 **Falstaff** sent **Henry V** a **Pint of Ale**, some **Dirty Puns**, and a **Lusty Wench**.

> **Henry V**: That's nice, but you can't send those to people unless you're frie . . .
>
> **Henry V**: Nope. Still don't know him.

♟ **Henry V** created a **Distraction**! He's diverting attention from the raging civil war by reclaiming parts of France.

🪖 **Henry V** is ignoring a **Request to Compromise**.

● **Henry V** would like his friends to go once more unto the breach.

🪓 **Henry V** is **losing friends** due to the **war** he's waging, his **betrayal**, and his **sentencing them to be hanged**.

> **Henry V**: This is really hard! I'd rather be a slave. Then I wouldn't have to make any decisions.

✉ **Henry V** sent **God** a **Kindly Ignore What My Dad Did to Get This Empire** request.

● **Henry V** won!

> **Henry V**: And we were outnumbered like five to one!

💘 **Henry V** changed his **Relationship Status** to "Married to French Princess."

● **Henry V** is boning up on his French.

> **Henry V**: Sorry. Force of habit.

● **Henry V** thinks we're on the right path now. How could my son screw it up?

This account now belongs to Henry VI.

✒ **Henry VI** added "King of England" to his **Work Info**.

> **Henry VI**: Though I really wouldn't have chosen this profession.

 Henry VI is losing this round of **Land Grab**! Thanks to him, England is gradually being kicked out of all the land his father worked so hard to win in France.

 Henry VI is adding **France** to his **Places I'm Told to Visit**.

> **Henry VI**: And they've got Joan of Arc now? How do I compete with that?

? **Henry VI** received the **Quiz: What Color Rose Would You Be?**

> **Henry VI**: I really don't get why everyone's always talking about roses around here. Wars and roses. Strange.

● **Henry VI** wonders why the Duke of York is sitting on my throne.

> **Henry VI**: Tell you what. I'll give you the throne when I die. My heirs won't be needing it.

● **Henry VI** is not a good father or king or person, or so I'm told.

> **Henry VI**: And now York is dead? And his kids want the throne? It's all just so complex.

Can someone draw me a diagram or something? And can I get some info on this Richard I keep hearing about?

- **Henry VI** will just wait in this tower locked up till you figure it all out.

  Henry VI: Oh, YOU'RE Richard. Weren't you at the thing with the . . .

This account now belongs to Richard III.

- **Richard III** says boo! Did I scare ya?

- **Richard III** is not yet the king, but just you wait.

- **Richard III** had a long, cold winter of unhappiness, but now my family is sooo happy. My brother Edward is the king. Isn't that great? Good for HIM.

- **Richard III** sent you a **Smile**.

  Richard III: Or am I just so DEFORMED, so UGLY, that you can't tell I'm smiling. Oh, I'm smiling. I'm definitely smiling.

- **Richard III** added "Blasphemous Rumors" to his **Playlist**.

- **Clarence** has been locked up, probably bound to die!

  Richard III: My brother Clarence. Yep, I made that happen.

- **King Edward** thinks Clarence's death is all his fault and is dying of guilt!

  Richard III: Oh, Eddie. I did that too.

- **Richard III** is now married to **Lady Anne**.

  Richard III: And I killed her husband! God, I'm good.

- **Richard III** can't hear you cause I'm killing everybody!

  Richard III: In fact, that little prince who's supposed to inherit the crown? Dead too. Also, his brother. Yes, I kill children now.

 Richard III doesn't understand why I don't have friends. I mean, I don't understand why I don't have friends. Who?

Richard III dead dead dead bad dreams whatsis? Who? Oh, this can't be good.

Richard III gets it now. You're not supposed to just kill people. Kind of wreaks havoc on your psyche.

Richard III will just fight this Richmond guy since everyone seems to think he's so great.

Richard III is not doing well. I'm losing the battle, and signs have been pointing to my death for DAYS, and now I don't have a horse. What I wouldn't give for a frickin' horse.

England became a fan of **The Tudors**.

● **Jonathan Swift** is satirizing scientists of the day like Robert Boyle and Isaac Newton!

● **Gulliver** says see, yeah, nobody gets those jokes anymore.

✳ **Gulliver** added **Wacky Places Like Glubbdubdrib**, **Luggnagg**, and **Japan** to his **Places I've Visited**.

● **Gulliver** will take England over having to do math any day.

Gulliver reviewed his **Recent Vacation**. He gave **Laputa** 2 out of 5 stars.

"Yeah, the good news about Laputa is not so many other tourists are there since it's off the ground and all. And they let me conjure up dead people. Got to talk to Aristotle! The bad news is they're a bunch of science geeks. What kind of society renounces right angles? They're just sooo smart and intellectual. So superior and great that you can barely have a conversation with any of them. And, okay, they made me feel like a dumbass."

● **Gulliver** just can't resist the high seas. I'm a ship captain now!

● **Gulliver** MUTINY. LEFT BEHIND ON ISLAND WITH SCARY CREATURES.

● **Gulliver** is fighting off bizarre-looking animals that are trying to defecate on him.

> **Gulliver**. Seriously, what's with the poo?

● **Gulliver** is watching horses act like people.

● **Gulliver** thinks a horse just called him a "Yahoo."

● **Gulliver** thinks the horses, er, Houyhnhnms, are so much better than the humans, er, Yahoos.

● **Gulliver** is trying to leave the group **Humankind**.

● **Gulliver** is being forced to go back and be part of **Humankind**.

● **Gulliver** is stopping up his nose with rue, lavender, and tobacco leaves because his family is so foul-smelling and terrible.

Gulliver reviewed his **Recent Vacation**. He gave **Houyhnhnmland** 5 out of 5 stars.

"Can't even talk about it. It was just so great. Me and the Houyhnhnms. They're so smart and cool. And now I'm just surrounded by Yahoos. Now if you'll excuse me, I'll be out in the stable with the horses having some REAL conversations. God."

Places I Think I've Been

A Farewell to Arms

NEWS FEED

 Lieutenant Henry joined the group **Americans Who Join the Italian Army Because They Happen to Be in Italy**.

● **Rinaldi** would like Henry to help him impress Catherine Barkley.

> **Henry**: No.
>
> **Rinaldi**: Yes.
>
> **Henry**: All right.

(image) **Henry** and **Catherine** are now friends.

● **Catherine** is talking about a boy who is dead.

> **Catherine**: Have you ever loved anyone?
>
> **Henry**: No.
>
> **Henry**: You have beautiful hair.

 Henry and **Catherine** are now in a relationship.

● **Henry** put his arm under Catherine's arm.

 Catherine sent **Henry** an **Open-Hand Slap**.

> **Catherine**: You are sweet.
>
> **Henry**: No, I'm not.
>
> **Catherine**: Be good to me, darling.

● **Catherine** and **Henry** are walking, and now they are stopping.

> **Catherine**: Have you come back? Because you were away, and now you've come back.

> **Henry**: I went away, but I'm back now, and I will always come back after going away.
>
> **Catherine**: Oh, I love you so.

● **Henry** does not love Catherine, but this is better than the whores.

 Catherine sent **Henry** a **Tired Kiss**.

 Catherine sent **Henry** a **Reluctant Hug**.

● **Henry** is fantasizing about going with Catherine to a hotel in Milan where they would drink and it would be hot and they would love each other all night in the hot night in Milan.

● **Henry** can't see Catherine tonight.

 Henry was sent **Loneliness** and **Yearning**.

 Catherine sent **Henry** a **Saint Anthony Medal**.

● **Henry** is in a dugout drinking rum with soldiers and wondering if they will be attacked.

● **Henry** is risking his life to get cheese.

● **Henry** saw a flash and heard a roar and tried to breathe, but his breath wouldn't come, and he felt himself rush bodily out of himself. Also, he hurt his leg.

● **Henry** is in the hospital and in a lot of pain.

● **Henry** became a fan of **Cognac**.

● **Henry** became a fan of **Brandy**.

● **Henry** became a fan of **Sherry**.

● **Henry** became a fan of **Grappa**.

● **Henry** became a fan of **Wine**.

● **Henry** VERMOUTH. A LOT OF VERMOUTH.

Catherine is in Henry's hospital room.

 Catherine is playing **Paradise by the Dashboard Light**.

> **Catherine**: Do you love me? You do love me, don't you?
>
> **Catherine**: Do you?
>
> **Henry**: Oh, darling, darling, darling.

Henry is now in love with **Catherine**.

 Henry is having a lovely time in the summer with Catherine.

 Catherine is listening to the rain and hopes Henry loves her and the rain won't make any difference because she is afraid of the rain and she will love Henry. In the rain.

 Catherine is going to have a baby.

> **Henry**: All right.
>
> **Catherine**: Oh, darling, we really are the same one and we mustn't misunderstand on purpose because people misunderstand and then they aren't the same one when they were the same one before they misunderstood.
>
> **Henry**: Nothing will come between us because you're brave and the coward dies a thousand deaths, the brave but once. Who said that?
>
> **Catherine**: I don't know. Who said that?
>
> **William Shakespeare**: I know! I know!
>
> **Catherine**: Cowards know a great deal about cowards, but the cowards don't know about being brave, and the brave die, but they don't talk about it because they're not cowards. The brave. We're splendid people.
>
> **Henry**: All right.

 Henry received **Drinking-Induced Jaundice**.

Henry received a **Return-to-the-Front Order**.

> **Catherine**: We always will be together.
>
> **Henry**: Except when I have to go away.

● **Henry** is going away. In the rain. Now it stopped raining, and it's kind of a mist. Now it's raining. Now there's a storm. Now it's just raining again.

Hemingway became a fan of **Using a Neutral, Disinterested Tone to Heighten the Realism of War**.

Hemingway sent **Henry** the **Fits and Starts of War** application, putting **Henry** in a column that stopped. It started again, then stopped. Several hours later, it started again, moved a few yards, then stopped. Then it started again.

● **Henry's** car is stuck in the mud.

Henry received **Friendly Fire** from **His Own Troops**.

● **Henry** and the soldiers might just be _____ed.

● **Henry** has been seized and interrogated for treachery in the rain.

● **Henry** is running away and jumping in the river in the rain.

● **Henry** is floating, pulling himself out, stripping off his medals, crawling under a canvas onto a train, getting his forehead gashed open, and waiting for the blood to congeal. Oh, and in the rain.

● **Henry** just turned down some grappa, so you know it's bad.

Henry left the group **The Italian Army**.

● **Henry** is in civilian clothes feeling like a masquerader.

● **Henry** will look for Catherine but will drink all this wine and grappa first.

Henry wrote on **Catherine's Wall**.

> *"A man often wishes to be alone, and a girl wishes to be alone too, and if they love each other then they get jealous of that, but we don't feel that, and sometimes when*

I was with girls I was more lonely with them than I would have been alone, but we are never lonely and never afraid when we are together and not alone."

 Catherine and **Henry** are attending **Switzerland via Rowboat**.

? **Henry** chose "Swiss Rain" over "Italian Rain" in the **Survey: If You're in a Hemingway Novel and It's Obviously Going to Rain Anyway, What Kind of Rain Would You Pick?**

 Henry and **Catherine** received **Pleasant Lives in Switzerland**.

 Henry sent himself a **Growing Papa Beard**. In just four days he'll look ready to hunt and fish while intoxicated.

> **Henry**: Oh, darling, I love you so.
>
> **Catherine**: Don't we have a fine time?
>
> **Henry**: We have a fine time and a good life and I love you and I'm crazy about you. You know I once had gonorrhea.
>
> **Catherine**: I wish I'd had gonorrhea so I could be like you.
>
> **Henry**: Oh, darling. Let's talk about your hair again.

● **Henry** long ago became a fan of **Detachment**, **Stoicism**, and **Aloofness**, but this love thing has kind of changed that.

● **Hemingway** is writing something that should never be read by any woman who plans on giving birth.

 Henry is once again a fan of **Detachment**, **Stoicism**, and **Aloofness**. And **Not Fighting in Wars**. Or **Loving Anyone Ever**. In the rain.

Ernest Hemingway
PROFILE

Basic Information

Networks: Ketchum, Key West, Bimini, Paris, Havana, España, the Great Expanse of My Mind

Hometown: A place full of ignorant hypocrites I've renounced forever (though please keep my contact info for the next reunion)

Relationship Status: Married to . . . wife five? No, just four, I'm told.

Personal Information

Interests: The hunt, the sea, safari, a little more champagne please, saying "How do you like it now, gentleman?" or whatever my favorite phrase is at the time over and over until it annoys all you sons of bitches, pugilists, the Heroic Code, a lovely vat of Chianti, the goddam science of war

Groups

Member of: All My Homes Are Now Museums, Breeders of Six-Toed Cats

Wall

 Ernest Hemingway tried to tell about the night and the day and how the night was better unless the day was very clean and cold, and he could not tell it.

 Ernest Hemingway sent you an **I Love You Hug** even though he does not love you nor has any idea of loving you.

Ernest Hemingway would really like you to call him "Papa" but can't seem to get the goddamn program here to do it. The imbeciles.

> **F. Scott Fitzgerald**: Hey, I'll call you Papa, Papa.
>
> **Ernest Hemingway**: Scottie! Let's go to the Dingo Bar and talk about that moronic Midwest. Just don't bring that wife of yours. I'd like to flambé her and throw her out with the marlins.
>
> **F. Scott Fitzgerald**: Can't today, Papa. Gotta give another *Gatsby* interview. People just love that book!
>
> **Ernest Hemingway**: GREAT! Good for you.

 Ernest Hemingway removed **F. Scott Fitzgerald** from his friend list.

 Ernest Hemingway will now talk Indian talk. Me write book and book good! Ha!

> **William Faulkner**: True Hemingway! As long as you've got the verbs and nouns in there, you don't need any other flowery language, say with three whole syllables or anything.
>
> **Ernest Hemingway**: When on earth did I accept your friend request?
>
> **William Faulkner**: I believe it was at that group party for Intoxicated Important American Writers.
>
> **Ernest Hemingway**: OOOOOH, such big words! In-tox-i-ca-ted. How DO you do it?
>
> **William Faulkner**: Papa, Papa. Yes, you never have used a word that might send a person to a dictionary.

Ernest Hemingway removed **William Faulkner** from his friend list.

Ernest Hemingway became a fan of **The Bulls**.

Ernest Hemingway thanks you for pointing out his arm is bleeding, but he hasn't had feeling there since 1933.

> **Gertrude Stein**: Who are you talking to?
>
> **Ernest Hemingway**: Oh, someone was asking me about that the other day, or year. I'm pretty sure.

Ernest Hemingway sent **Ezra Pound** a **Hug** and a **Playful Punch in the Stomach**.

 Ernest Hemingway is decorating his **Wall** with **Swordfish**.

 Ernest Hemingway likes animals better than most human beings. Or, he should say shooting animals more than shooting most human beings.

> **Marlene Dietrich**: Oh, Papa, people aren't so bad, no?
>
> **Ernest Hemingway**: Oh, you sweet old Kraut. I like my cat Boise.
>
> **William Faulkner**: Not a person, Ernie.
>
> **Ernest Hemingway**: Faulkner! You burnt-up piece of okra. How'd you get back on my page?
>
> **William Faulkner**: You invited me back and I couldn't resist.
>
> **Ernest Hemingway**: Intoxicated Important American Writers?
>
> **William Faulkner**: Intoxicated Nobel Laureates.
>
> **Ernest Hemingway**: Nobels! Damn Swedes.

 Ernest Hemingway says leave the sons of bitches alone and they are liable to start crawling back into the womb or somewhere if you drop a porkpie hat.

> **Zelda Fitzgerald**: HEMINGWAY! You FREAK! What's with you unfriending poor Scotty and friending me?? Ya big PERVERT. You're just so jealous of him SOOOO SOOOO jealous of his FAME. BOOOO. BOOOOO. Hey, can we borrow a few grand to have a swell party on the roof of the Dingo Bar? ROOOOF! ROOF!!!!!!
>
> **Ernest Hemingway**: I have got to stop signing in to this place.

Quiz:

Which Dystopia Are You In: *1984*, *Brave New World*, or Social Media?

Pick the words that make sense to you:

A)   Doublethink, Oceania
B)   Centrifugal Bumble-Puppy, Hypnopaedia
C)   SuperPoke, Scrabulous

The enemy is:

A)   The Brotherhood
B)   The Truth
C)   Your Friend's Angry Vampire

To be rebellious you:

A)   Make a facial expression
B)   Get married
C)   Join a group called 1,000,000 Against [thing that really annoys you]

When a person doesn't conform to your society, he:

A)   Becomes an "unperson"
B)   Is exiled to a distant island
C)   Gets "blocked" or "de-friended"

A memory hole is:

A)   A slot in your cubicle leading to a giant incinerator that will eliminate historical errors
B)   Something sexual, probably
C)   The process of trying to dig up any recollection of that total stranger who just sent you a friend request

Nature is:

A) The what now?
B) A place you go with expensive transportation to play expensive "country sports"
C) Something you can save by sending cute-faced plants to all your friends

The leaders of your society know what you want because:

A) Your behavior is being monitored through telescreens
B) You were conditioned as an infant to want these things
C) Your online behavior is being monitored to better target advertising

Your history is:

A) Being "rectified" to account for predictions that turned out to be wrong
B) Completely irrelevant to what you need to fulfill a craving right now
C) Being revisited through embarrassing high school photos posted by your "friends"

Control is:

A) Something you willingly give up to the Party because it knows what's best
B) Something you're conditioned to give up because it's the basis of a happy society
C) Something you willingly give up so you can add an application that lets you send a drawing of a martini to one of your friends

Sex is:

A) Only to be used as a means of producing new Party members
B) Not necessary for reproduction, but you should go have a lot of it with a lot of different people right now!
C) Something you should take a quiz about to determine your favorite position

New life comes as a result of:

A) Doubleplus ungood sexual intercourse
B) "Decanting" technologically produced infants out of specially designed bottles
C) A mysterious egg sent to you by a friend that will soon hatch to reveal a cuddly animal

You love:

A) Big Brother
B) Our Blessed Ford
C) It's complicated

Your society is divided into:

A) Inner Party, Outer Party, and proles

B) Alphas, Betas, Gammas, Deltas, and Epsilons

C) Top Friends, Friends, People You May Know, and People You Choose to Ignore

Thinking is:

A) Not recommended

B) Something you don't have time for because you're so *soma*ed out and happy

C) What you need to unscramble these letters to make a series of words. You've got three minutes, GO!

You are whipped into a frenzy by:

A) Two Minutes Hate

B) Two minutes without *soma*

C) That friend who updates her status every freakin' two minutes

Photography and visual arts:

A) Should be doctored for the benefit of the Party's message

B) Should be used to make "feely" films

C) Should be doctored to make you look like you have a hairstyle from the 1970s

Freedom is:

A) Slavery

B) Not necessary when you can have all the sex you want

C) Just another word for nothing left to lose (or so says your Favorite Quotation)

Shakespeare is:

A) A forbidden word you woke up with on your lips after having an erotic dream

B) The kind of thing you should steer away from if you want to be a good citizen

C) An inspiration for many, many a book, including the one you're holding

Your Dystopia:

If you chose mostly A, congratulations, you're in the world of *1984*! Nothing feels more like home to you than the all-powerful dystopia of the Thought Police, the Party, Newspeak, and the face-eating rats of Room 101. It's a world that spawned the word *Orwellian*, not to mention seasons and seasons of a ubiquitous reality show. Feel good in the knowledge that two plus two makes five and that Oceania has always been at war with Eastasia . . . Eurasia? . . . no, always with Eastasia. And you've always loved Big Brother. Of course you have. Was that a glimmer of independence in your eye? We didn't think so.

If you chose mostly B, the World State of *Brave New World* is more your thing. You've been conditioned since you were an embryo to play exactly the role in society you do today. You see no need for religion, art, families, or even Shakespeare because Mustapha Mond and his fellow World Controllers have made sure you get all the sex and drugs you need to be part of a stable, content, and completely passive society. But watch out for those Savages from the Reservation. They have crazy ideas about learning and emotions and giving birth and—gasp!—*loving* each other that could throw things completely out of whack. We're cringing just thinking about it. Woops, thinking? Why would we do that?

If you chose mostly C, you've become entrenched in the world of **Social Media**! You've stopped communicating with actual people to spend more time updating your status, tending your virtual farm, pretending you're in the mafia, and writing comments on the pages of people you haven't seen in person since kindergarten, if ever. What's that? Your boyfriend wants to *talk* to you? Just tell him you will as soon as you take these quizzes on what your birthday means about you, what kind of shoe you are, and what kind of dog breed you'd be. Go ahead, we're always here for you. Always, always here.

Animal Farm's Napoleon and Charlotte's Web's Wilbur Play Scrabulific!

S	O	M	E	P	I	G
			Q			
			U			
		P	A	L		
			L			

SMACK TALK!

Napoleon: Somepig? Somepig? What's that?

Wilbur: That's a word I put on your "equal." I thought after you made fun of me so much for starting with "pal," I'd use something a bit more complex.

Napoleon: But what's somepig?

Wilbur: I know it's a word because Charlotte wrote it in her web.

Napoleon: Who's this Charlotte you keep talking about? One of the farm workers you've subjugated under your supreme power?

Wilbur: NO. She's my ffff . . . WAAAAAA SNORT SNORT.

Wilbur: She was my friend. She passed away and . . . WAAAAAA SNORT OINK.

Napoleon: What the hell are you doing?

Wilbur: I'm sorry! I'm crying because I miss my friend!

Napoleon: Your "pal"? Hehe. I'm sure she died for the greater good. Or perhaps because she was causing some problems for your leaders and had to be *taken care of*.

Wilbur: You really don't know anything about me, do you?

Napoleon: No, you friended me. And since I've got all those morons in the barn doing all the work, I've got nothing better to do than drink and play games, like any other person.

Wilbur: You're not a person. You're a pig.

Napoleon: Am I, though? Am I?

Gone with the Wind

NEWS FEED

Scarlett O'Hara is crushing on Ashley Wilkes.

 **Scarlett** threw a **Scarlett** at **Ashley**! **Fan yourself, heave your bosom at, rustle your petticoat**, or **do something else**.

Ashley and **Melanie Hamilton** are now married.

Scarlett and **Charles Hamilton** are now married.

Charles joined the group **The Confederate Army**.

Scarlett changed her profile to **Widow with a Baby**.

Scarlett is helping Melanie have a baby.

Prissy doesn't know how to help a woman through childbirth.

The South rejoined the group **The USA**.

Scarlett's mother is dead, her father is crazy, and Tara's a mess.

Scarlett will plan her meals more carefully from now on.

Scarlett has a new use for curtains.

Scarlett's sister **Suellen** is now engaged to **Frank Kennedy**.

Scarlett is now married to **Frank Kennedy**.

Scarlett had another baby.

Scarlett's father found a fatal error in the **Horse-Riding** application.

Frank found a fatal error in the **Gettin' Revenge 'n Protectin' the Women** application.

Scarlett is now married to **Rhett Butler**.

Scarlett had another baby, Bonnie Blue Butler.

Bonnie should really not be adding the **Horse-Riding** application.

Rhett's mind is currently offline.

Melanie found a fatal error in the **Be a Sweet and True Woman** application.

Melanie sent **Scarlett** a **Deathbed Look-After-Ashley** request.

Scarlett is, HOLD EVERYTHING, in love with Rhett! Who knew?

Scarlett sent **Rhett** a **Love Me** request.

Rhett hit **Ignore**.

Scarlett will try again tomorrow.

Lord of the Flies

GROUP

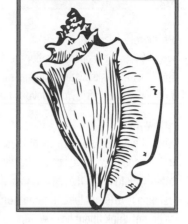

The Flies' Twentieth Reunion!

Basic Info

Type: Student Groups/Alumni Groups

Description: Look, I know we technically weren't all in "school" together, but we certainly got "schooled"! Am I right?

What to bring: Large seashells, matches and kindling wood, highly selective memories

Recent News

Hey all—

It's been way too long, guys. And I know some of you have traveled far from England (or are just hermits here because speaking to other people is too big a reminder of the failure of human society we demonstrated—I hear ya).

But I'd love to see all your faces again . . . now not so covered with warrior paint and blood! Let's meet up! We could go up to Blackpool Beach and build some huts lol. Or just go to the pub near my place and decorate it with an island theme? Leis, drinks in coconuts, the whole bit. Meanwhile, let's hear what you've been up to all this time! And let me know if there's anyone missing from the group. Some people I swear have fallen off the face of the earth. (Or off a cliff after being hit by a boulder. Ha! Too soon?)

Hope to hear from all of you! So many memories. How 'bout: Kill the beast! Cut his throat! Spill his blood! Do him in! LMAO

Jack

Wall

Phil wrote

A lot of you might not remember me. I was a littlun? I think I peed myself at one assembly talking about the Beastie! I'm assistant regional manager now for an airplane parts company. Ironic, isn't it? So great to "see" you all here. Would love to meet up sometime too. Should I bring the roast pork? Ha ha.

Eric wrote

Hiya, it's Eric. I know, it was always "Samneric," on account of my twin, you know, Sam. He's kind of indisposed now. Or you could say he hasn't stopped drinking since we got back cause he's found no other way to make the nightmares stop. Kidding! Well, a little bit. I was kind of down for a while too, especially after all the attention from our story getting out kind of died down and there was nothing to do but think about how we turned into primordial creatures with no sense of human decency. I'm an accountant now. Wife and four boys—I could have my own "mini-tribe" here at home!

Roger wrote

KILLLLLLLLLL! Too great. I could not BELIEVE it when I heard from my boy Jack about this thing. We used to ROLL back in the day. Or at least I'd gladly stick my spear up a sow's anus if he told me to! What did I do with all my fame and glory? Truthfully, got a plumbing and appliance repair business. You probably saw the adverts: "I was Roger, from *Lord of the Flies*, now I'm King of the Loo." Not too glam, but I can get you a discount on washer/drier combo units. Just say whether or not you were with Jack's group. Joke! If you weren't, you're likely dead, eh? Cheers.

Jack wrote

Seeing as I started this group (and used to rule you all with an iron fist! rofl), I should tell you what I've been up to. As you know, I worked the circuit after our story got out: the chat shows, that huge book deal for my memoir (too bad the Madness made it impossible for me to write back then), my stint on *Survivor*—can you believe they voted me off on the second episode? "The tribe has spoken." Since when do tribes get to "speak"? And no hunting? Running across a series of balance beams carrying giant puzzle pieces and then building a map of Colombia and putting it on a scale that raises a flag and lights a fire, but no dance circles leading to the death of a pig? Idiots. Since then, been laying low, developing a *Flies* animated series, and working on my new men's fragrance, "Slaughter." Keep the posts coming!

Ralph wrote

Hello.

Jack wrote

Ralphie boy! Didn't think you had the gonads to join us! JK. Glad you're here. I know we went through some SHITE together, dude, but it was so long ago. We can laugh about it now, right? So what are you doing now? Running your own company? Wouldn't be surprised. Probably still yelling at everyone for not cleaning up after themselves and chasing after each other with spears.

Ralph wrote

Hello, Jack. My wife saw this page and thought it might be good for me to try to talk to you a little bit. ANGER PIG PIGGY.

Ralph wrote

I'm sorry for that. Things are going well. Thank you for asking.

Jack wrote

Ralph, honestly, so glad you're here. All in the past, right? So do you keep in touch with anybody? Whatever happened to that Simon guy who was always talking to plants?

Ralph wrote

Well, the group mistook him for the "beast," ripped him apart with their teeth and bare hands, then you knocked Piggy off the cliff with the rock, lit the jungle on fire, and tried to have the tribe spear me to death on the beach. THAT. Happened to Simon.

Jack wrote

Right! And then the naval officer showed up and hauled us all outta there. Man, your memory's better than mine! I mean we were all kind of off our nut by then, yeah? You gotta admit you were too. Always going off about the almighty conch and the bloody fire.

Ralph wrote

I'm SORRY for wanting a FIRE so we could be RESCUED. HEAD PIG MOUTH.

Jack wrote

Oh! Yeah. Forgot that too. But that fire in the jungle did the trick!

Percival wrote

Hi, mates! I still think about those sunsets and the insect noises that sometimes masked the sound of small boys weeping.

Ralph wrote

What I want to know, Jack, is how you can sleep at night. I mean that chain of spear-your-own-wild-game restaurants? The "Flies Boys Experience" summer camps? And that, GOD, that Piggy brand of eyewear? I can't even FIRE FIRE CONCH can't even conceive what goes through your head.

Jack wrote

Dude, you haven't changed at all. How about living in the moment? Which reminds me, just got a deal to work as a script advisor on *Lost*. Oahu, baby! So I won't be able to meet up anytime soon, unfortunately. But if you get together, be sure to take some photos for me, K? And don't forget your Chief, now. Or I'll f-ing scratch your bloody eyes out. Ha! I'm so kidding. Man, I miss those days. Peace out.

Don Quixote

NEWS FEED

NOTIFICATION:

Your friend **Matt** has **dropkicked** you! **Check it out**! OR **adopt a pet with**, **hug**, **play twister with**, or **do something else** back!!

- **Don Quixote** says how dare that person Matt dropkick you! I forswear vengeance against Matt and his ilk and will now joust with him.

- **Don Quixote** says joust with me, Matt, joust! With your purported dropkicking expertise and your vile photo in which you appear witty and yet approachable!

- **Don Quixote** asks why won't you speak, Matt? You who dropkicked my good friend, you will not go unpunished! It is my service to God to wipe your wickedness from the face of the earth!

- **Don Quixote** is appalled that now Matt b@!$#slapped you! He b@!$#slapped you? Come, Sancho! Ride your ass quickly and help me defend this fair maiden against cruel, cruel Matt.

- **Don Quixote** wonders how Matt can be casually updating his favorite quotes when he has harmed our friend by kicking her, quite possibly to her certain death!

- **Don Quixote** says if she survived the dropping, she may not do as well with the kicking! And, oh, the slapping in addition to the dropping and the kicking! We must hurry, Rocinante, my brave steed. Run, my stallion.

- **Don Quixote** does not know what granny panties are but does not think Matt could have anything true or virtuous in mind by "rocking" them with you.

- **Don Quixote** calls Sancho! Sancho! Have you seen all of the people that Matt has violated? He just achieved a new "level" because of all the dropkicking and b@!$#slapping and panty-rocking he is doing! Sancho! I cannot do this alone!

- **Don Quixote** cannot believe that Matt has taken to THROWING BARNYARD ANIMALS at our friend. Animals, Sancho! What if he tries to throw dear Rocinante here? Not that he could because Rocinante is such a fierce, fierce steed. In fact, Rocinante is so overpowered with his own fierceness he has trouble staying upright.

Don Quixote is Oh, oh no. Not this, Matt. Matt has spanked you? In the name of the princess Dulcinea del Toboso, he will not get away with spanking you! His black arts shall avail him little against the goodness of my sword!

Don Quixote wants to know who these people are who are becoming "friends" with Matt after they have seen what he does to you! Perhaps they are other knights sworn to protect you and need to get closer to him to stop him from committing these terrible acts of violence.

Don Quixote declares, oh, heed, new friends of Matt! Do not succumb to his charms! He does not just want you to "drink cocoa" or "get your hair did" with him! Soon he will be shooting you with a taser gun and leaving you for dead while injured barnyard animals squeal in agony at your feet!

Don Quixote suggests you keep your bumper stickers and flair strongly fortified as I engage nefarious Matt in a fierce and unequal battle! And for God's sake keep him out of your little garden! Hide your Happy Hibiscus as I drag Matt's entrails across the cold, cold ground.

Don Quixote is down! He's down! Not injured, and even if he was, you would not hear him complain, as he is a heroic knight errant! But oh, it is not enjoyable being on one's side in the mud with an old horse stepping on one's helmet.

Don Quixote was sent a **Bouquet of Flowers** for Dulcinea del Toboso, a **Bag of Feed** for Rocinante, a **Horse** for Sancho, and a **Medal for Bravest Knight Errant in All the Kingdom** . . . by Matt.

Don Quixote says come Matt, you are most fortunate to have won the right to see the deeds I will now display.

Don Quixote wonders if maybe Matt could teach me this dropkicking thing? It might be just the weapon I need to fight the giants with the many, many arms that circle all day and night, seemingly at one with the wind.

Don Quixote will defeat them one day, Matt. I will.

Quiz:
Are You a REAL MAN?

Ernest Hemingway **took the** Are You a Real MAN? **quiz with the result:**
40% . . . You could stand to get to the gym once in a while.

People you're compatible with: Ashley Wilkes, Ishmael, Jonathan Swift, Ron Weasley

People who thrashed you! Try again to beat their score: Fyodor Dostoyevsky, Queequeg, Don Quixote, Joseph Conrad, Squealer the Pig

COMMENT

Ernest Hemingway: This is ridiculous. Of course I'm a REAL MAN, ask anyone.

Joseph Conrad: Clearly not. This was a very thorough and accurate test.

Ernest Hemingway: I'm the Old Man and the Sea! I drove an ambulance in World War I! I've run with the bulls! Or at least been in a lovely second-story café where you can sort of see the running of the bulls. I have no idea how I ended up losing to you wusses.

Joseph Conrad: I traveled into the HEART OF DARKNESS of deepest Africa!

Ernest Hemingway: Yeah, but I was in a plane that crashed into the African bush . . . Twice! You went there on what, a boat?

Ishmael: Boats can be scary.

Ernest Hemingway: The point is I've done plenty of manly things.

Fyodor Dostoyevsky: Have you ever been in a Siberian prison camp? Or been told you're going to be shot by firing squad and then you stand there, and stand there, and stand there, and then they don't do it?

Squealer: And have you walked on your hind legs? That's hard.

Queequeg: And I eat people.

Ernest Hemingway: This is crazy! And come on, I'm supposedly less of a man than Don Quixote? For one thing, he's wearing a washing basin on his head.

Don Quixote: How dare you assail the integrity of my battle garments!

Ernest Hemingway: I'm just saying, anyone can see I'm a REAL MAN compared to a guy fighting imaginary monsters on a horse that's almost dead. And I certainly shouldn't be thrown in with Ishmael and Pretty Boy Ashley.

Ashley Wilkes: I indeed wish I could be a better man. For my Melanie. And for Scarlett. Oh, my heart is always torn apart so that I can never make a decision. I can't even decide what to eat for lunch.

Ernest Hemingway: You SEE? This test proves nothing. I am leagues above you people. LEAGUES.

Ashley Wilkes: I mean, I was leaning toward roast beef, but chicken salad does sound good.

Don Quixote: No one shall disparage my manhood! We must joust now!

Joseph Conrad: The Congo! Darkness! African stomach ailments!

Fyodor Dostoyevsky: Exile! Starvation! Very cold temperatures!

Ernest Hemingway: Lord! What a bunch of pansy-ass idiots. Now, if you'll excuse me, I've got to go wrestle a wildebeest. Or something.

Ernest Hemingway: And how do I retake this thing?

And now, the **Man versus Society Network** presents . . .

Abridged News Feeds for Books About Man and Society That People Pretend to Have Read to Impress Others

Crime and Punishment

- **Raskolnikov** is murdering Alyona Ivanovna and her sister with an ax.

- **Raskolnikov** received eight years of hard labor in Siberia, and he's sorry he did it.

War and Peace

- **Napoleon Bonaparte** is attempting to control all of Europe, including Russia, and this is affecting many different people in Russia.

- **Napoleon's** army did not succeed in invading Russia and had to retreat, leaving Russia alone.

Gravity's Rainbow

- **Tyrone Slothrop** is excited! Unfortunately, whenever he gets an, ahem, excitement like this, a V-2 Rocket is fired.

Les Misérables

- **Jean Valjean** is just out of jail after serving nineteen years for stealing bread and for trying to escape multiple times!

- **Jean Valjean** is realizing life outside of jail in nineteenth-century France can also be hard.

Heart of Darkness

- **Joseph Conrad** is not a fan of **Imperialism**.

    > **Marlow**: Yeah, it's this really scary thing. What's the word I'm looking for?
    > **Kurtz**: Horror. The horror.
    > **Marlow**: Right.

5

Dr. Jekyll is a changed man.

The Evil That Men Do Network

Macbeth • Edgar Allan Poe • The Metamorphosis • Frankenstein •
The Strange Case of Dr. Jekyll and Mr. Hyde • Dracula

Macbeth

NEWS FEED

- **The Witches** think fair is foul and vice versa.

- **King Duncan** thinks Macbeth deserves a promotion.

- **The Witches** think Macbeth will get a promotion and get to be king.

- **The Witches** think Banquo will produce a whole line of kings.

- **Macbeth** thinks The Witches should repost that Macbeth-being-king part.

 Lady Macbeth sent **Macbeth** a gift: the **Cojones to Kill Duncan**.

Duncan invited himself to attend **Dinner at the Macbeths'**.

> **Lady Macbeth**: In that case, I'd like some cojones too, please.

 Macbeth added the **Moral Quandary** application.

> **Lady Macbeth**: How bout adding the **Man Up Already** application?

- **Lady Macbeth** would like Macbeth to screw his courage up like a tuning peg, or like something to do with a crossbow, or who knows, just some kind of place where you stick things, and get his ass in gear, ya big chicken.

> **Macbeth**: But.
>
> **Lady Macbeth**: Bawk, bawk, bawk!

- **Macbeth** hopes they never have any daughters.

 Macbeth was sent a piece of **Hallucinatory Medieval Weaponry**.

- **Macbeth** is killing Duncan. And the ability to ever sleep again.

● **Macbeth** says oh, no, the king is dead.

> **Lady Macbeth**: Oh, how could it be in our house and everything, oh, no.

● **Malcolm** thinks he and Donalbain should take a nice trip to Far Away from Here.

● **Donalbain** suspects people are hiding things behind their cheerful dental work.

● **Macbeth** added "King of Scotland" to his **Work Info**.

● **Macbeth** sent the System Administrator a **Banquo and Fleance Removal** request.

● **Banquo** signed off, but **Fleance** is still online.

> **Macbeth**: Eek!
>
> **Lady Macbeth**: Can you act normal please?

● **Macbeth** will act normal as soon as Dead Banquo gets out of my chair.

● **The Witches** say here comes trouble.

 The Witches sent **Macbeth** a **Horoscope**.

> *Somebody has been thinking about you! (HINT: rhymes with "dick-muff.") And it's probably not in a nice way. But don't worry, none of woman born can hurt you. Also, you can relax until the forest meets the hill.*

● **Macbeth** says I'm totally safe! Better massacre Macduff's family anyway.

● **Macbeth** joined the group **Killers Who Are Doing It Just for Fun Now**.

 Lady Macbeth joined the group **People with Obsessive-Compulsive Disorder**.

 Lady Macbeth joined the group **People with Batty Murderess Sleepwalking Disorder**.

● **Lady Macbeth** could use a good stain remover.

● **Lady Macbeth** found a good Lady-Macbeth's-life remover.

- **Macbeth** thinks life is just an idiotic story that drags on and on.

 Macbeth received a **message**.

   The forest is coming toward us, sir.

- **Macbeth** would like his life to drag on a little longer.

- **Macbeth** still has that whole "of woman born" thing going for me, right?

- **Macduff** doesn't want to get into seventeenth-century semantics, but his mother had a C-section.

- **Macbeth** says oh, hell, bring it on Macduff.

- **Macduff** took **Macbeth's Headshot**. Or, no, that would be his head.

> **Malcolm**: Phew! Glad this whole Curse of Macbeth thing is over.
>
> **Macduff**: Yeah, we'll never hear about that again.
>
> **Malcolm**: Nope. All done.

Witch #3's Photo Album: My Family

In this photo:
Witch #1, **Witch #2**, **Witch #3**

COMMENT

Witch #2: That's horrible! Why'd you have to post this one?

Witch #1: Yeah, what am I doing with my face? Am I drunk?

Witch #2: Where were we? That bog doesn't look remotely familiar. And I look like I have five chins.

Witch #3: It's from our Scotland trip, remember? We were so obliterated!

Witch #1: Look at #2 in that pic. She's like, "Dude, what's with my thumbs? They keep pricking."

Witch #2: I was exhausted! That Macbeth guy had us up all night making up crap.

Witch #1: Right! What a jackass.

Witch #3: Well, people believe what they want to believe.

Witch #1: Seriously, what is my face doing? Am I talking? Am I hacking something up?

Edgar Allan Poe
PROFILE

Basic Information

Networks: Charm City, The Beyond

Relationship Status: Incessant Woe

Personal Information

Interests: Intemperance, the grotesque, my thirteen-year-old cousin, Germans, Coleridge, paying the rent, absinthe, the occasional opium, imaginary friends, premature burial, rum, your pale blue eye, insisting I'm sane despite all evidence to the contrary, gruesome mysteries, PERVERSENESS, medieval torture methods, goth girls, carnies, loving with a love that is more than love

Favorite Movies: *Saw* (I–V)

Favorite Music: Heart, My Bloody Valentine, The Killers

Favorite Songs: "Paranoid," "Somebody's Watching Me," "Someone to Watch Over Me," "Don't Stand So Close to Me," "Every Breath You Take," "Creep"

Friends: Dr. Faustus, Ray Lewis, Alice Cooper, John Waters, Usher

Wall

 Edgar Allan Poe is reading a quaint and curious volume of forgotten lore.

 Edgar Allan Poe wonders if you hear that too.

 Edgar Allan Poe is considering the low, stifled sound that arises from the bottom of the soul when overcharged with awe.

Edgar Allan Poe received a **ROFL Catz**:

 Edgar Allan Poe sent **Bad Karma** to Everyone.

 Edgar Allan Poe sent you a **Cask of Amontillado**.

"At least I'm pretty sure that's what it is. It would really help if you would taste it to make sure, down deep in my family's catacombs. No, I'm not still mad at you."

Edgar Allan Poe is pretty sure your sister was dead when we buried her.

The Old Man gave Edgar the **Vulture Eye**! Terrorize, dismember, bury beneath the floorboards, or break-dance with The Old Man.

Edgar Allan Poe will go in there, but why don't you go first?

Edgar Allan Poe joined the group **Yeah, I'm a Loser, and What Literary Genres Have YOU Started?**

Edgar Allan Poe became a fan of **The Spanish Inquisition**.

Edgar Allan Poe was napping when you came rapping and so faintly tapping, tapping on his chamber door.

Edgar Allan Poe just reached a new milestone. He's choked more than **fifty people** with his bare hands.

Edgar Allan Poe thinks the orangutan did it.

Edgar Allan Poe just stabbed himself by accident.

Edgar Allan Poe is not nervous. Why do you ask?

Edgar Allan Poe wrote on your **Wall**. Then he buried someone in it. Then he made it and another Wall start closing in on you. Then he started bragging about it to the police. Then he ran around the room screaming and tearing his hair out.

Edgar Allan Poe will not stop looking at you that way.

The Metamorphosis
NEWS FEED

 Gregor Samsa received an **Involuntary Profile Change**.

> **Gregor**: Yeah, I seem to have a shell now.
>
> **Gregor**: Also, I'm dark brown.
>
> **Gregor**: And shiny.
>
> **Gregor**: Twitchy too.

 Gregor received **Many, Many Legs**.

> **Gregor**: I wonder if I should call in sick.

 Gregor received a **Knock on His Door**.

 Gregor sent his **Mom** and **Dad** an **Inappropriately Loud Chirping Noise**.

● **Gregor** tried to get up and slammed himself full-throttle into the bedpost.

● **Gregor** will just sit here for the indefinite future.

● **Gregor** could rock back and forth for a while maybe? Get some momentum going?

> **Gregor**: Crap. Doorbell.

 Gregor's office sent **Gregor** an **Annoyingly Officious Clerk**.

> **Clerk**: We know Gregor is always irresponsible and lazy, but him being fifteen minutes late today is beyond the pale.
>
> **Gregor**: Blah, blah, negligent. Blah blah obstinate. Blah pointless. Blah poor performance.

● **Gregor** is wondering what's worse: being a bug or having my crappy job?

Gregor sent a **Mouth Finder** request.

> **Gregor**: Well, it's hard to hold a key in your mouth if you don't know where it is.

Gregor got the door open!

> **Gregor**: Now, as you can see, I'm not feeling well.
>
> **Gregor**: Mom, you okay? Mom's passed out on the floor. Dad? Please stop crying. A-hole clerk? Right, he's screaming and running down the stairs.

 Gregor's Dad sent **Gregor** a **Stick Prod** and a **Slap with a Rolled-Up Newspaper**.

> **Gregor**: Humiliating.
>
> **Gregor**: And now I think I squashed part of myself.

 Gregor received a **Bowl of Milk** from his sister **Grete**.

> **Gregor**: That's nice. Though I wish the taste of it didn't make me want to regurgitate my innards.

Gregor became a fan of **Garbage**.

> **Gregor**: This is my thing now, I guess.

 Gregor added "squeezing under furniture," "running around on the ceiling," and "trying to count my eyes" to his **Activities**.

 Gregor excreted something on his **Family's Wall**.

> **Gregor**: Sorry.

Gregor sent his **Mom** a **Series of Fainting Spells**.

Gregor's Dad sent **Gregor** a **Dozen Rapidly Hurled Apples**.

> **Gregor**: Really? Ow ow owwww!
>
> **Gregor**: Owwww! Ow!
>
> **Gregor**: Ow.

● **Gregor** is happy his family is doing okay without him.

> **Gregor**: I guess.
>
> **Gregor**: Though it would be nice to have food besides the apple stuck in my back. Which I'm pretty sure is infected.
>
> **Gregor**: And smells.

● **Gregor** thinks it's nice his family is taking in boarders to help pay the bills.

> **Gregor**: Oh, and what's that? Grete playing the violin?
>
> **Gregor**: How lovely! Maybe if I just crawl out there, I can watch a little bit.

The Boarders left the **Samsa Family** network.

Gregor's Family is playing **Conversation**! They're talking about how the bug can't possibly be **Gregor**. And how if it really was **Gregor** it would have left them alone in peace.

> **Gregor**: Well, SORRRRY!
>
> **Gregor**: I guess I'll just sit here and feel sorry for myself and the way my family treats me, like I'm Franz Kafka or something.
>
> **Gregor**: And . . . A-WUMP.

Gregor removed his **Exoskeleton** from his profile.

> **Gregor**: Well, now I hope you're happy.

Gregor's Family upgraded their **Virus Protection Software**.

Frankenstein
NEWS FEED

 Dr. Frankenstein became a fan of **Weird Science**.

 Dr. Frankenstein created a new application, **Second Life**.

 The Monster sent **Dr. Frankenstein** a **Menacing Glare**.

 Dr. Frankenstein received **Breathless Horror** and **Disgust**.

 Dr. Frankenstein received **Endless Shivers** and **Some Horrible Gothic Illness**.

 The Monster sent **Dr. Frankenstein** an **Even More Menacing Menacing Glare**.

 Dr. Frankenstein is UNDO UNDO UNDO UNDO.

 Dr. Frankenstein is hoping it was all a dream!

 Dr. Frankenstein has a trashed apartment, dead brother, and what's that thing . . .

> **The Monster:** Hi.
>
> **The Monster:** Yeah, not a dream.

 Justine is being blamed for forcibly removing Victor's brother from the system.

 Justine received a **Public Execution**.

 Dr. Frankenstein isn't sure how this could get any worse.

> **The Monster:** Hello there, let me tell you how this could get worse.

 The Monster is now "Looking for a relationship."

 Dr. Frankenstein suggested a friend for **The Monster**. She will accept his friend request just as soon as he can get her online.

 The Monster sent **Dr. Frankenstein** a **Blood-Tingling Smile**.

Dr. Frankenstein is DELETE DELETE DELETE DELETE.

 Dr. Frankenstein removed the **Random Body Parts Collection** from his page.

 Dr. Frankenstein received a **Notification** that he killed his own best friend.

 Dr. Frankenstein updated his profile to **Raving Mad and in Prison**.

> **The Monster**: See, this is the getting worse part.

 Dr. Frankenstein and **Elizabeth** are now married.

 The Monster became a fan of **Wedding Crashers**.

 Elizabeth is screaming on her wedding night and not in a good way.

 Dr. Frankenstein changed his **Relationship Status** to "Vengeful Widower."

 Dr. Frankenstein removed "bodybuilding" from his **Interests**.

 The Monster removed "having people who care about me" and "playing God" from **Dr. Frankenstein's Activities**.

 Dr. Frankenstein and **The Monster** are playing **Dogsled Chase**! **Dr. Frankenstein** won this round by getting rescued and telling his whole awful story before his account was deactivated.

 The Monster added **Victor's Deathbed** to his **Places I've Been**.

The Monster added the song "You Always Hurt the One You Love" to his **Favorites**.

The Monster removed "Research Subject" from his **Work Info**.

Frankenstein's Monster

PROFILE

Basic Information

Location: Wandering to the Ends of the Earth in Sadness

Birthday: Don't MOCK me

Relationship Status: You are MOCKING ME, I know you are MOCKING ME

Personal Information

Favorite Music: "The Rising," "Monster," "Thriller"

Favorite TV: *Nip/Tuck*

Favorite Movies: *Alive, Invasion of the Body Snatchers, Body Double, Night of the Living Dead, Young Frankenstein* (at least I get to dance in that one), *Live and Let Die*

Favorite Books: *Paradise Lost,* "The Rime of the Ancient Mariner," Mary Wollstonecraft, Ovid, *Dracula* (I know we're always thrown in together, but I do find him interesting)

Wall

 The Monster could really use a name so everyone would stop calling him "The Monster."

> **The Monster**: And no, my name isn't Frankenstein.

 The Monster has never met Abbott and Costello. Nor any "Wolf Man."

The Monster wonders why no one has tagged him yet in their self-obsessed chain letters. He might want to write a self-obsessed chain letter too you know.

 The Monster is human (sort of), and he needs to be loved, just like everybody else does.

The Strange Case of Dr. Jekyll and Mr. Hyde

NEWS FEED

- **Dr. Jekyll** is not himself these days.

- **Dr. Jekyll** is a changed man.

- **Dr. Jekyll** can see things from both sides.

- **Dr. Jekyll** is feeling conflicted.

 Dr. Jekyll and **Mr. Hyde** are playing **Bribe**! **Dr. Jekyll** will write you a **BIG CHECK** if you forget about the little girl **Mr. Hyde** trampled in broad daylight. What little girl, you ask? Congratulations! **You've earned 100 quid**.

- **Mr. Utterson** doesn't approve of Dr. Jekyll's new friend and hopes he doesn't try to friend him too.

> **Dr. Jekyll**: Oh, I don't think he'll be doing that. DEVIL DEVIL DEVIL FIEND.
>
> **Mr. Utterson**: Why, that's quite curious behavior.
>
> **Mr. Enfield**: Yes, curious. But we are proper gentlemen, and we don't go about gossiping.
>
> **Mr. Utterson**: Of course not. Quite true.

Dr. Jekyll wrote on **Mr. Utterson's Wall**.

"Haven't seen you for a long spell! I know, I've been kind of out of commission I"

Dr. Jekyll wrote on **Mr. Utterson's Wall**.

"Thanks for going to the dinner party. Glad you liked the lamb and"

Dr. Jekyll's Playlist:

"Within You, Without You"
"The Scientist"
"Always on My Mind"
"Right by Your Side"
"You Really Got a Hold on Me"
"Two of Us"
"Double Vision"
"Love Potion #9"

Dr. Jekyll wrote on **Mr. Utterson's Wall**.

"Yes, the weather has been pleasant! London in the spring is so"

Dr. Jekyll wrote on **Mr. Utterson's Wall**.

"I'm sorry I keep getting interrupted and can't seem to finish a"

Dr. Jekyll finds you annoying and would like to club you to death.

> **Mr. Utterson**: That doesn't sound like you, Jekyll.
>
> **Dr. Jekyll**: Ha. Joking!

Dr. Jekyll will club you right now.

Mr. Utterson finds all of this kind of bizarre.

Dr. Jekyll posted a **Note**.

I'm very sorry to have killed the people and will go now, bye. Yours, Mr. Hyde.

> **Dr. Jekyll**: See! No more Mr. Hyde around here.

 Mr. Utterson is playing **Strange Coincidences**!

Is there any significance to the facts that:

Dr. Jekyll's friend, Dr. Lanyon, just died from some sort of shock?

Dr. Lanyon left a letter to be opened only after Dr. Jekyll's death?

Mr. Hyde's handwriting is exactly the same as Dr. Jekyll's?

Mr. Hyde has been seen around town in too-big, Dr. Jekyll—like clothes?

Mr. Utterson answered: "No, there isn't any significance. And it's not very fitting for me to wonder about my friend's personal affairs anyway."

Terrible Job! Mr. Utterson's score inducted him into the **Worst Detectives Ever Hall of Fame**.

 Dr. Jekyll changed his profile picture.

 Dr. Jekyll changed his profile picture.

 Dr. Jekyll changed his profile picture.

 Dr. Jekyll changed his profile picture.

 Dr. Jekyll updated his **Last Will and Testament**.

 Dr. Jekyll blocked all access to visitors.

Mr. Utterson invited **Mr. Enfield** to attend a **Sociable Walk**.

> **Mr. Utterson**: Why, there's Dr. Jekyll in his window! Hello, old friend.
>
> **Dr. Jekyll**: I don't feel so good. GOOD BAD EVIL FIEND DEATH AAAAWK!
>
> **Mr. Utterson**: Well that was again quite strange, but we shouldn't talk about such unusual behavior.
>
> **Mr. Enfield**: Yes, let's obsess about it quietly in our own minds.

Dr. Jekyll sent **Mr. Utterson** a **Strange New Voice from Behind the Door**.

Mr. Utterson is breaching **Dr. Jekyll's** security settings.

Mr. Utterson received a **notification**.

> **Mr. Hyde** won a game of **Murder/Suicide**! Click here to play too!

Mr. Utterson received a **Whodunit Package**.

> **Mr. Utterson**: Oh good, then Dr. Jekyll must still be alive even though this Hyde person, in Dr. Jekyll's clothes, is dead on the ground with all these documents prepared by Dr. Jekyll that says I should read them, and that I should read Dr. Lanyon's letter, even though that was only in the case of Dr. Jekyll's death. Oh, everything should be fine.

Dr. Lanyon posted a **Posthumous Note**.

> *Mr. Hyde, Dr. Jekyll = Same Person. Crazy inner demon potion. Scared me to death.*

Dr. Jekyll posted a **Posthumous Note**.

> *It's all true. It was fun for a while. But then it wasn't.*

● **Mr. Utterson** learned Dr. Jekyll was leading a double life.

● **Mr. Utterson** learned Dr. Jekyll had a dark side.

> **Mr. Utterson**: Oh! I get it now! How odd! And how depraved! Let's not talk about it anymore.
>
> **Mr. Enfield**: Yes, let's not.
>
> **Mr. Utterson**: Okay, maybe let's talk about it a bit more, for like another century and a half. Or so.
>
> **Mr. Enfield**: Yes, let's do.

Dr. Jekyll and Mr. Hyde play Scrabulific!

P	L	E	A	S	U	R	E
			N				
			A				
			R				
			F				

SMACK TALK!

Dr. Jekyll: Oh, Hyde, I do enjoy playing Scrabulific! with you. I just never know what you're going to do next!

Mr. Hyde: Mwahaha! Snart Snarf.

Dr. Jekyll: You slay me! You've got me ROFL. Or ROF anyway. Man, I've got a headache.

Dracula

NEWS FEED

 **Jonathan Harker** posted a **Note**.

> The real estate law practice is going awesome! My first gig is to go to Transylvania (!!) to get this guy to settle an account. Ha! A count! Might have to stay a few days, but in this climate, we have to do what we have to do, right? Hope he doesn't bleed me dry.

● **Jonathan** is on a long journey.

🪭 **Jonathan** became a fan of **The Carpathian Mountains**.

● **Jonathan** wonders why every time he mentions where he's going someone hands him a crucifix.

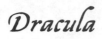 **Jonathan** posted a **Note**.

> Met the Buyer. Have to say the ride there creeped me out. Wolves kept howling, we were going in circles, and I swear my driver had a see-through body. But the count is perfectly pleasant, just kind of odd-looking. Pointy teeth. I told him he'll like the place he's buying in England: a spacious fortress on twenty acres bordering an insane asylum.

Jonathan posted a **Note**.

> So this is weird. Cut myself shaving and the count lunged at me! Maybe he wanted my crucifix? And he didn't have a reflection in the mirror, which, by the way, he threw out the window. I would go get it, but it seems the doors are locked and I'm a prisoner now.

Jonathan posted a **Note**.

> Okay, I probably shouldn't write this since my fiancée Mina might see it, but I woke up to three gorgeous but immensely strange women slithering around. The count

showed up and made them stop, threw them a bag, and said something about a half-smothered child being in it? Seriously.

Dracula received **Wooden Boxes** filled with earth! He's almost collected them all!

Dracula is crawling up the side of the building wearing Jonathan's clothes.

Jonathan is watching a woman outside get devoured by wolves.

Jonathan posted a **Note**.

Don't know what to say here. Found the count sleeping in one of the boxes of dirt. Those freaky women keep hanging out by my room. The count told me I could leave, then sicced wolves on me. Tried to kill him with a shovel. Didn't. Think I'm kind of screwed.

Mina wrote on **Lucy's Wall**.

"Can't wait for Jonathan to come back!"

Lucy wrote on **Mina's Wall**.

"Now we're both engaged! Just fancy, I got proposed to by three guys today! Quincey's an American stereotype, Dr. Seward runs a lunatic asylum, and Holmwood is the one I picked. Dear Mina, why are men so noble and perfect when women are so despicable and worthless?"

Mina wrote on **Lucy's Wall**.

"I don't know, sweet Lucy! What kind of women are we?"

Lucy wrote on **Mina's Wall**.

"One-dimensional virginal Victorian women, I think!"

Seward is refocusing his feelings for Lucy the Pure on Renfield, the homicidal maniac.

Renfield became a fan of **Spiders**, **Flies**, and **Sparrows**.

Renfield just spit up a bunch of feathers.

> **Seward**: Oh my!

Renfield wants a kitten!

> **Seward**: I don't think so.

Mina is having fun with Lucy in the eroding, eerie seaside abbey.

Mina posted a news story.

> *Whitby Dailygraph*
>
> **Unmanned Ghost Ship, Crates of Dirt Arrive to Harbour**
>
> *Horrified Dead Captain Strapped to Tiller*

Lucy became a fan of **Sleepwalking**.

Mina found Lucy in the churchyard with holes in her neck.

> **Mina**: I'm sure you just scratched your fragile virgin skin by accident.

Lucy is updating the size of her **Neck Holes**.

Mina found Jonathan raving in Budapest.

Renfield found Dracula's new house and is now humping the door.

Van Helsing joined the **England** network.

Van Helsing thinks Lucy looks drained.

Van Helsing sent **Lucy** a **Garlic Necklace** using **Folksy Talismans**.

Lucy's Mother better get rid of those horrible-smelling flowers.

> **Van Helsing**: Gott in Himmel!

● **Lucy** is now on death's door.

Lucy posted a **Note**.

> *Gee, I'm feeling so much better. All of my suitors have been giving me their blood—so I'm just an innocent maiden getting shot up with liquid from virile men. I feel like I just woke up from a bad dream to find sunshine and rainbows and big, strapping men. Did I mention the men?*

Lucy posted a **Note**.

> *Not good now. Something kept flapping by the window. Then a giant wolf jumped through it. Mom died of fright, of course. I blacked out. Servants freaked and started drinking wine, which was drugged or poisoned or something. Now I'm alone. Dizzy. And, of course, still very innocent and virginal. What will become of me?*

 Lucy received more **Manly Liquid**.

 Lucy sent **Holmwood** a **Ravish Me** request.

 Lucy joined the group **The Undead**.

> **Holmwood**: Oh, my dear Lucy! My love!
>
> **Van Helsing**: Ya, sorry about that. Now let's stuff a crucifix in her mouth and cut off her head.

Van Helsing posted a news story.

Westminster Gazette

Local Tots Have Ball Recounting Crazy-Lady Neck-Sucking

New pastime has kids in a tizzy! They talk of a "Bloofer Lady" who wanders the graveyard, tries to eat them, and leaves them for dead. Great fun, but the town recommends keeping pets and particularly cute babies indoors.

Van Helsing says we must stop her!

Van Helsing invited **Seward**, **Quincey**, and **Holmwood** to an **Old-Time Vampire Slaying**.

Holmwood drove a stake through Lucy's heart like Thor with his hammer, his untrembling arm rising and falling, driving deeper and deeper till the blood spurted up into the night.

> **Mina**: How distressing! Good thing pure, sweet Lucy isn't here to witness it.
>
> **Mina**: Oh, right.

Mina joined the group **Sane People Who Happen to Live in a Mental Hospital**.

Renfield thinks Mina's looking drained. Oh, not fair, master!

Van Helsing found Mina kneeling on the bed, licking blood off Dracula's chest.

> **Renfield**: SO not fair!

Dracula is really tired of you British and is so out of here.

Van Helsing invited his posse to **Old-Time Vampire Slaying II: The Master**.

Van Helsing and his posse are chasing **Dracula** back to **Eastern Europe**!

The Virile British Men sent **Dracula** a **Stake Through the Heart**.

Dracula joined the group **The Dead Dead**.

Everyone (besides the dumb American) defied the typical gothic horror story and lived happily ever after.

The Evil That Men Do Network

DISCUSSION BOARD

Dr. Frankenstein wrote

My app is not doing what it's supposed to do. In that, it is supposed to bring me fame and God-like status and is instead ripping the heads off people.

Dracula wrote

Yeah, I can't get my "vampire" application to work. First of all, I don't understand how it "fights" other vampires by me clicking a button. Second, I keep losing.

The Monster wrote

I'd like to clarify my portrayal in numerous "adaptations" of which people are "fans." I don't stick my arms straight ahead of me and grunt. I'm quite literate, actually; I'm right now reading *Plutarch's Lives* and *Paradise Lost*, which has some fascinating parallels.

Gregor wrote

I'm still a bug over here.

Dracula wrote

And why is my vampire dressed like a "sexy Catholic schoolgirl"?

Dr. Jekyll wrote

My new application is also having problems. I tried entering the OOOPH

Dracula wrote

Who is this "Edward" guy? Other people I DON'T know: Sookie Stackhouse, Bella Swan, Buffy, Tom Cruise, Brad Pitt, Kiefer Sutherland, The Sesame Street Count.

The Monster wrote

Hear, hear! I do not know a Herman Munster, and I don't think his wife Lily or this "Grandpa" know anything about real vampires.

Dracula wrote

Thanks, man. Now can you tell me why my vampire would want to fight a zombie? Do zombies even have blood? And why would a zombie carry cheerleading pom-poms?

Gregor wrote

Um, yeah, on my back, legs moving uselessly. Parents ignoring me. Want to die.

Watson wrote

Holmes, can you help these gentlemen? It seems they have many different mysteries that could become Adventures for you.

Sherlock Holmes wrote

My dear Watson, there are only so many times I can be revived after falling into a gorge locked in mortal combat with Professor Moriarty.

Dr. Jekyll wrote

Time to kick you all in the face! What? Sorry.

Gregor wrote

I think my eyes are molting.

Dracula wrote

In this Vampire game, if I get 20,000 vampire dollars, I can dress up in a chicken suit. What on earth does that mean?

The Monster wrote

Can we just talk about the travesty that is Franken Berry? And Boo Berry? BOO Berry?

Dracula wrote

Why would I want to buy garlic? I'm a VAMPIRE.

Deathmatch Quiz!

Match the writer of classic literature with his or her own ending!

1) Joined the group **Men Who Should Have Used Protection**

2) Joined the group **Men Who Might Be Found Wandering Around Sick and Delirious in Someone Else's Clothes**

3) Joined the group **Maidens Who Should Avoid Catching Cold with All That Tuberculosis Going Around**

4) Joined the group **Men Who Are Not Bulletproof**

5) Joined the group **Women Not Good with Mercury**

6) Joined the group **People Who Shouldn't Leave Their Wives at Age Eighty-Two and Go Traveling**

7) Joined the group **Men Who Should Have Joined the Group Alcoholics Anonymous**

8) Joined the group **People Who Probably Should Stop the Nonstop Speaking Engagements After Surviving That Horrific Train Crash**

9) Joined the group **People Who Come and Go with Halley's Comet**

10) Joined the group **Maidens Who Don't Float**

A)	Mark Twain	F)	Charles Dickens
B)	Emily Brontë	G)	Edgar Allan Poe
C)	Leo Tolstoy	H)	Ernest Hemingway
D)	Virginia Woolf	I)	F. Scott Fitzgerald
E)	Gustave Flaubert	J)	Louisa May Alcott

Answer Key: *1) E, 2) G, 3) B, 4) H, 5) J, 6) C, 7) I, 8) F, 9) A, 10) D*

6

Humbert changed his Relationship Status to "It's complicated."

The Mischief-Makers Network

Puck's Live Feed • Lolita • Lady Chatterley's Lover • Oscar Wilde

Puck's
LIVE FEED

 Puck changed your security settings. 11:59 p.m.

 Puck sent an annoying email to all of your friends, saying he was you. 12:01 a.m.

 Puck made all of your status updates very large, flashing, and upside-down. 12:13 a.m.

 Puck had you fling a thong at your boss. 12:24 a.m.

 Puck posted a private message from your boyfriend on your Wall. 1:05 a.m.

 Puck replaced all of your photos with that sixth-grade one where you have headgear and a perm. 1:16 a.m.

 Puck set it to send you a notification every time one of your friends says the word *and*. 1:45 a.m.

 Puck made you send a friend request to your ex-boyfriend's new wife. 2:12 a.m.

 Puck invited all of your friends to be on the "ground floor" of your pyramid scheme. 2:27 a.m.

 Puck earned your lowest score ever on **WordJumble**. 2:33 a.m.

 Puck made your **Werewolf** eat his own arm. 2:41 a.m.

 Puck infested your **Small Fertile Square** with rabid squirrels. 2:44 a.m.

 Puck had you dedicate "My Heart Will Go On" to your weird uncle. 3:02 a.m.

 Puck invited your mother to join and then made all your status updates about how much you like heroin. 3:09 a.m.

 Puck set it so whenever your friends look at their profile pages, a Rosie O'Donnell head pops up and shrieks. 3:26 a.m.

Puck posted a video of you being mean to a puppy. 3:41 a.m.

 Puck made your favorite destination "Up Ur Butt." 3:57 a.m.

 Puck set your **Language** to "Drunken Slur." 4:08 a.m.

 Puck made you throw **Real Sheep** at everyone. 4:19 a.m.

 Puck made you become a fan of **Sewage**. 4:21 a.m.

 Puck made your **Favorite Book** *Gonorrhea and You*. 4:39 a.m.

 Puck made your **Relationship Status** "Married to Goat." 4:55 a.m.

 Puck made you join an actual mob war. 5:17 a.m.

 Puck made you comment "Losers!" on photos of your friends' children. 5:23 a.m.

 Puck sent you **Woodbine**, **Sweet Musk Roses**, and **Eglantine**. 5:34 a.m.

 Puck gave you the **Head of an Ass**. Wait, no, you already had that! Ha ha. 5:49 a.m.

 Puck is sorry you no longer have friends. 5:52 a.m.

 Puck is kidding! Not sorry at all. 6:00 a.m.

Lolita
NEWS FEED

Humbert became a fan of **Girls My Age If This Was Twenty-five Years Ago**.

Humbert added "bouts of insanity" to his **Activities**.

Humbert joined the **Ramsdale** network.

Humbert has no interest in staying at this house owned by Charlotte Haze.

Dolores "Lolita" Haze, Charlotte's daughter, is a person **Humbert** may know.

Humbert updated his **Home Address**.

Humbert thinks Lolita is graceful with the tart grace of her coltish subteens.

Humbert thinks Lolita's little doves seem well-formed already.

Lolita added "swimming" to her **Interests**.

> **Lolita**: And I also like boating and magazines and ice cream sundaes!!! ☺☺

Humbert changed his **Relationship Status** to "It's complicated."

Humbert's little cup is brimming with tiddles.

WARNING

> **Message from Admin**: *Our systems indicate you've been using terms and subject matter deemed inappropriate for our site. Misusing our features may result in your account being deactivated. Thank you.*

Humbert is just excited about life today.

Humbert is especially excited to sit here while Lolita eats an apple.

Humbert added "Babysitter" to his **Work Info**.

> **Humbert**: But only for girls under fourteen, preferably with hips no bigger than a squatting lad's.

 Humbert joined the group **People Who Really Shouldn't Keep a Journal**.

 Lolita is adding the town of **Climax** to her **Cities Where I've Gone to Summer Camp**.

 Charlotte wrote on **Humbert's Wall**.

> *"I love you I love you my dearest, dearest, mon cher, cher monsieur."*

 Humbert is considering child custody laws, should he get married.

 Charlotte and **Humbert** are now married.

 Charlotte added "sneaking through my new husband's stuff" to her **Interests**.

? **Humbert** challenged **Charlotte** to the **Most Likely Scenario** quiz.

From this journal you found, which of these do you think is really going on?

> —*Your husband is obsessed with your underage daughter.*
>
> —*Your husband hates you and married you just to be close to your underage daughter.*
>
> —*Your husband has a lively imagination and those are just notes for a novel!*

● **Charlotte** is screaming at Humbert and running out into the street.

● **Charlotte** is feeling run down.

● **Charlotte** joined the group **Women Not Able to Stop Moving Vehicles with Themselves**.

● **Humbert** is inly moaning, inly dying.

● **Humbert** is Lo-lee-ta. Lo. Lee. Ta.

● **Humbert** is Lola. Dolly. Dolores. Lolita.

● **Humbert** is Lo.

- **Humbert** is Lolita, Lolita, Lolita, Lolita, Lolita, Lolita, Lolita, Lolita, Lolita, Lolita, Lolita, Lolita, Lolita, Lolita, Lolita, Lolita, Lolita, Lolita, Lo

 WARNING

> **Message from Admin:** *The subject matter and terms used in your applications continue to appear inappropriate. Also, writing a name over and over again for 300 status updates in a row is just weird. Please refrain from misusing (and being weird with) our applications, or your account will be deactivated. Thank you.*

- **Humbert** is getting Lolita in Climax.

WARNING

- **Humbert** is angry that Lolita would prefer a Hamburger over a Humburger.

COME ON NOW

 Humbert added **Lolita** to his **Family Tree** as his **daughter**.

 Humbert invited **Lolita** on a **Terrible Road Trip to Nowhere**.

> **Lolita**: I think I'll vomit if I look at a cow again.

Humbert became a fan of **Functional Motels**.

> **Lolita**: Oh you dirty, dirty old man!

 WARNING

> **Message from Admin**: *Okay, this is just crazy. First, there's the questionable terminology on your own profile, including your **Interests** ("insatiable illicit love," "constant amorous exercise," "when a nymphet gropes under my bench for a lost marble").*
>
> *But there are also your multiple requests to have your "daughter's" (quotation marks yours) profile removed from the system, unless she declines all friend requests from "any kind of male" and from girls whose profile pictures are "disappointing."*

We're going to have to go ahead and deactivate your account and suggest you stay away from this site (and, for the love of God, from your "daughter") for the near future, barring requests from the psychoanalytical community to use your information for research purposes. Thank you.

Lolita was **Kidnapped!** by the famed playwright and child pornographer, **Clare Quilty**. **Lolita** escaped with the **Ol' He Got Bored of Me** trick.

Lolita is now married to **Dick Schiller**.

Lolita is writing a note to her "Dad" about how broke she is and how she's pregnant and how much sadness and hardship she's gone through.

> **Some Random Guy**: Lolita, Lolita
>
> **Admin**: Oh, this won't end well for anybody.

Humbert Humbert Plays Scrabulific!

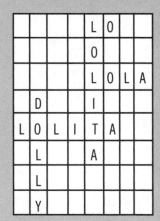

SMACK TALK!

> **Admin**: What did we tell you??
>
> **Humbert**: Okay, I'm going, I'm going.

Lady Chatterley's Lover

NEWS FEED

 Connie Reid is looking for someone to do.

> **Connie**: Ha! I meant something, of course. Very bored around here. Extremely bored. With the giant estate and impotent husband, Clifford. Woops! Important husband. He's a lord and all.

 Connie's restlessness is thrilling inside her body, in her womb.

 Connie's limbs are twitching when she doesn't want them to twitch.

Connie's spine is jerking when she doesn't want it to jerk.

Sir Malcolm recommended an **Activity** to **Connie**: "Find Yourself a Man-Friend."

> **Connie**: Thanks, Dad.

Connie is now friends with **Michaelis**, the Irish playwright.

 Connie received a **Terrible Appeal** from **Michaelis** and nearly fell over.

Connie is doing Michaelis.

> **Connie**: Well, I thought you wanted to know what I was doing right now.

Clifford recommended an **Activity** to **Connie**: "Have a Baby with Some Other Fellow and Give Me an Heir."

> **Connie**: Thanks, dear. But who?
>
> **Clifford**: Oh, look, there's our new gamekeeper, Mellors.

Connie thinks Mellors is being cold, aloof, mocking, and impudent.

> **Connie**: Who IS that guy?

Michaelis changed his **Looking for** to "Hopeless Affection" and "Essential Remoteness."

 Michaelis added "Finishing before Connie" and "yet not wanting Connie to finish after he's finished" to his **Activities**.

 **Connie** is no longer a fan of **Man-Friends**.

 Connie accidentally saw Mellors washing himself in the forest! His clumsy breeches slipping down over the pure, delicate, white loins, the bones showing a little, the sense of aloneness!

 Connie received a regular invitation to **Sit Around Talking About Nothing with Snobby Intellectuals**.

 Connie might just be hanging out in the forest some more.

 Clifford invited **Mrs. Bolton** to join the **Wragby** network.

 Mrs. Bolton added the **Infantilizing a Wealthy Gentleman** application.

Clifford had his **Manhood** removed from his profile. Both behaviorally and literally!

Connie sat against an erect, alive, powerful, elastic, young pine tree.

D. H. Lawrence became a fan of **Driving the Point Home, or So to Speak**.

Mellors is playing **Hard to Get**.

 Connie would like a key to the hut where Mellors hangs out just to, you know, hang out, too, despite that giant mansion over there.

> **Mellors**: If yer want ter be 'ere, yo'll non want me messin' abaht a' th' time.

Connie thinks Mellors is refusing to speak ordinary English just to mock her.

> **Mellors**: Me! Ah thowt it wor' ordinary.

Connie added the **Gradually Increasing Husband-Hatred** application.

 Mellors posted a **Link**: **A Wonderful View of Baby Chickens**.

 Connie was sent **Copious Unbidden Tears**.

 Mellors received a **Flame Shooting and Leaping Up in His Loins**.

 Mellors added **Connie's Peace on Earth of a Soft Quiescent Body** to his list of **Places I'd Like to Visit**.

> **Mellors**: For me it was good. Was it for you?

 Connie added "Lying" to her **Activities**.

Connie is, though, going back to the hut tomorrow.

Connie is clinging to Mellors, unconscious in passion and feeling the soft bud of him within her stirring, rhythms flushing up into her with a strange growing motion, swelling and beginning again the unspeakable motion that was not really motion.

Connie is feeling whirlpools of sensation swirling deeper and deeper through all her tissue and consciousness.

Connie is crying in unconscious inarticulate cries.

> **Humbert**: And you want to deactivate MY account?
>
> **Admin**: Well, we know it's dirty, but we're not exactly sure how.

 Mrs. Bolton posted a news story.

> *Lady Chatterley Trying to Have Baby Despite Husband's Lack of Baby-Making Ability*
>
> **Clifford**: Hurrah! I will try new baby-making technology!
>
> **Connie**: Hmm.

 Connie added **Coalmine Country** to **Places I Visited to Let the Author Voice His Thoughts on Industrialization**.

● **Connie** is speaking to Mellors in a funny accent.

● **Connie** and **Mellors** have named their genitals "John Thomas" and "Lady Jane" and are having them talk to each other.

> **Humbert**: Really? Really?
>
> **Admin**: We kind of want to see where this goes.

● **Mellors** is weaving flowers in Connie's maiden-hair and having a marriage ceremony for their genitals.

> **Humbert**: I give up.

✴ **Connie** added **Venice** to her **Cities I've Visited**.

🗔 **Clifford** wrote on **Connie's Wall**.

"Big gossip here! Mellors's wife is back, and he's going to be in trouble!"

🗔 **Mrs. Bolton** wrote on **Connie's Wall**.

"Mellors's wife is running around town saying he's cheating on her, can you believe it? She's violent and unpredictable and probably going through menopause."

🗔 **Mellors** wrote on **Connie's Wall**.

"The cat is out of the bag, along with various other pussies."

● **Connie** is wondering how being pregnant with Mellors's baby is going to play out in the Wragby network.

♟ **Connie** and **Mellors** are sharing a **Plan**: **Mellors** gets a divorce while **Connie** tells **Clifford** she loves **Duncan Forbes**.

♟ **Connie** failed completely in this **Plan** and will not go on to the next round.

● **Connie** is still waiting for her divorce.

- **Mellors** is still waiting for his divorce.

- **Clifford** has officially become a man-child.

 Mellors wrote on **Connie's Wall**.

> *"Don't worry, Clifford will divorce you. He'll eventually want to spew you out as the vile creature he thinks you are."*

- **D. H. Lawrence** wrote an ending without much of a climax, so to speak.

John Thomas sent **His Regards** to **Lady Jane**.

Quiz:

What Kind of Adulteress Are YOU????

Put these in order of things you'd be MOST LIKELY to LEAST LIKELY to do:

—Ask your lover to name your genitals and decorate them with flowers!

—Don't physically cheat (much) on your husband(s) but constantly think of another man whenever you make love!

—Have an affair but drag it out forever till the point you're shunned from society and pathetically needy!

—Mysteriously get pregnant while your husband is living in another country or possibly shipwrecked!

—Have an affair because your husband is impotent thanks to the war!

—Have affairs just because you're bored and kind of awful!

Comment

Lady Chatterley: I'd like to know how to file a complaint here? There is an item in this quiz obviously *loosely* based on me, and I don't feel I'm being fairly represented.

Anna Karenina: Me too!

Lady Chatterley: Which one are you?

Anna Karenina: I think I'm the "drag it out forever" person, which isn't really accurate. My husband wouldn't give me a divorce! That certainly puts a little stress on extracurricular action. Which one's yours?

Lady Chatterley: The impotent one, which is not correct at all. Yes, my husband had . . . difficulties after the war, but he's also an idiot. Plus, I really love my guy, Mellors.

Scarlett O'Hara: AND?

Lady Chatterley: And what?

Scarlett O'Hara: I declare, don't you have another item in that quiz?

Lady Chatterley: Um.

Anna Karenina: Oh, YEAH! You're flowers-strewn-around-your-privates woman!

Lady Chatterley: I hardly think that's the way it should be described.

Madame Bovary: LOL!! "Lady Jane." Right? What was the other one?

Anna Karenina: John Thomas!!

Lady Chatterley: Well, I'm SORRY. I guess I'm just too Twentieth Century for all of you.

Madame Bovary: OOOOH. Careful, she's going to sic John Thomas on us! And he'd be pretty fierce-looking if he wasn't decorated with forget-me-nots.

Lady Chatterley: Hyacinth and . . . I'm so sure! Which one are you in that quiz?

Madame Bovary: Don't be ridiculous! I'm not in that quiz.

Scarlett O'Hara: I beg to differ; I believe you're the "awful" one.

Madame Bovary: Okay, clearly we're all BORED with our husbands or we wouldn't be doing this. Except for Pilgrim's Progress over there. Shipwreck? That's your excuse?

Hester Prynne: I won't discuss it. It's between me And God.

Madame Bovary: Well, aren't YOU so perfect? Getting all BEDAZZLED on your potato-sack dress and getting that pastor to lose his frickin' mind. Great job with your nutjob of a daughter too.

Lady Chatterley: Oh, yeah. She's the awful one.

Anna Karenina: Definitely.

Oscar Wilde

PROFILE

Basic Information

Networks: Dublin, London, The Stage

Birthday: October 16, 1854

Relationship Status: Depends Who's Asking

Personal Information

Activities: Quipping

Interests: Not living within my means (anyone who does so suffers from lack of imagination), being talked about (the only thing worse is not being talked about), forgiving my enemies (nothing annoys them so much), being inconsistent (as consistency is the last refuge of the unimaginative), passing on good advice (it is never any use to oneself), getting into other people's business (my own business always bores me to death)

Favorite Quotations: Anything said by me

Wall

 Oscar Wilde can resist anything but temptation.

 Oscar Wilde thinks that God in creating Man somewhat overestimated his ability.

 Oscar Wilde thinks a little sincerity is a dangerous thing, and a great deal of it is absolutely fatal.

> **Mark Twain**: A man is never more truthful than when he acknowledges himself a liar.

> **Oscar Wilde**: Excuse me, are you quipping atop of my quip?
>
> **Mark Twain**: Appears so.

 Oscar Wilde is not young enough to know everything.

> **Mark Twain**: Age is an issue of mind over matter. If you don't mind, it doesn't matter.
>
> **Oscar Wilde**: Please refrain from doing that.
>
> **Mark Twain**: I really don't see why. People love my quotes. Put 'em all over their walls. Thought we could join up and they'd get two for the price of one.
>
> **Oscar Wilde**: I'd rather not.
>
> **Mark Twain**: Okeydoke.

 Oscar Wilde says when the gods wish to punish us, they answer our prayers.

> **Mark Twain**: Do the right thing. It will gratify some people and astonish the rest.
>
> **Oscar Wilde**: Please stop, or I'll block you from my status updates.
>
> **Mark Twain**: Do the thing you fear most and the death of fear is certain.
>
> **Oscar Wilde**: Quit it! Quit quipping!
>
> **Mark Twain**: K.

 Oscar Wilde thinks only dull people are brilliant at breakfast.

> **William Shakespeare**: Brevity is the soul of wit.
>
> **Oscar Wilde**: ???
>
> **William Shakespeare**: Saw you guys quipping and thought I'd join in. If music be the food of love, play on.
>
> **Oscar Wilde**: That doesn't have anything to do with anything. Also, it's not a quip, it's from a play.
>
> **William Shakespeare**: Quip, quote, whatever. The better part of valor is discretion.
>
> **Mark Twain**: It's not the size of the dog in the fight, it's the size of the fight in the dog.

William Shakespeare: Ha! Let me not to the marriage of true minds admit impediments.

Mark Twain: Let us live so that when we come to die even the undertaker will be sorry.

William Shakespeare: So true, so true.

Oscar Wilde: You guys are killing me here.

 Oscar Wilde says we are all in the gutter, but some of us are looking at the stars.

William Shakespeare: Good one! All the world's a stage, and all the men and women merely players.

Oscar Wilde: That's hardly fair. You practically invented the language.

William Shakespeare: I know! The course of true love never did run smooth.

Mark Twain: A man who carries a cat by the tail learns something he can learn no other way.

William Shakespeare: LOL!!

Oscar Wilde: There is no way you're laughing out loud at that. It doesn't even make sense.

 Oscar Wilde thinks we live in an age when unnecessary things are our only necessities.

Oscar Wilde: Arguments are to be avoided; they are always vulgar and often convincing. Whenever people agree with me I always feel I must be wrong. Life is far too important a thing to ever talk seriously about.

William Shakespeare: Oscar, you're going to injure yourself quipping. Also, you'll never win in a quip-off against me. We know what we are, but not what we may be. Neither a borrower nor a lender be. Frailty, thy name is woman!

Mark Twain: The coldest winter I ever spent was summer in San Francisco.

William Shakespeare: Har har.

Oscar Wilde: Who would even care about that quip unless they were in San Francisco?

Ernest Hemingway: How do you fellows find the time to quip so often? No one ever quotes my quips.

Charles Dickens: They do have bad writing contests in your honor, however, as well as those look-alike contests. No one does that for me.

Ernest Hemingway: You get built-in publicity every damn Christmas!

Charles Dickens: True.

Dorothy Parker: I hear we're quipping over here? I don't care what is written about me so long as it isn't true.

Oscar Wilde: Can you all take this somewhere else? This is my page. My quips.

William Shakespeare: Sure.

Charles Dickens: Of course.

Dorothy Parker: Certainly.

Ernest Hemingway: Damn right.

Mark Twain: Okeydoke.

 Oscar Wilde thinks one can live down everything except a good reputation.

William Shakespeare: Exit, pursued by bear.

William Shakespeare: Sorry, just had to. It's not a quip, just a stage direction. *Winter's Tale*.

William Shakespeare: That's all, I swear. Exit, pursued by bear. It's just funny.

William Shakespeare: Cause it's right there, in the stage directions. A bear.

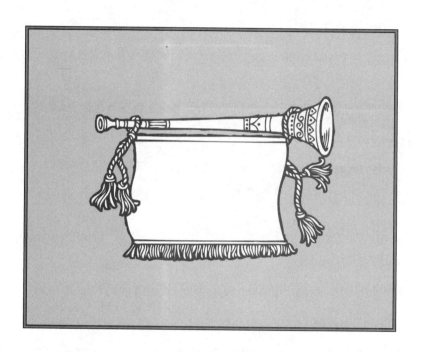

7

*Oedipus has some things to
talk over with the wife.*

The What a Piece of Work Network

King Lear • *Oedipus Rex* • *Of Mice and Men* • *Death of a Salesman* • *The Great Gatsby* •
The House of Mirth

King Lear

King Lear invited **Goneril**, **Regan**, and **Cordelia** to play the age-old parental game, **Prove How Much You Love Me**! You have just one chance to inherit part of the kingdom or be considered dead in your father's eyes.

> **Goneril**: I love you so so so much. SOOOOOOO much. I can't even put enough *O*s in my SOOOOO because I love you so much.
>
> **Regan**: Goneril doesn't have enough *O*s, but I do, I love you SOOOOOOOOOOOOOOOOO OOOOOOOOOOOOOOOOOOOOOOOOO much!!!!! You really can't even fathom how much I love you.

Goneril sent **Lear** 17 **Flowers**, 25 **Plants**, and 4 **Birthday Cakes**.

Regan sent **Lear** a **Martini**, a **Rum and Coke**, 45 **Vodka Tonics**, and a **New Cloak**.

Goneril sent **Lear** 40 **Magic Castles**, 500 **Bumper Stickers**, 7,984 **Happy Feelings**, and an **'80s-Style VW Convertible**.

⬤ **Cordelia** is not playing.

> **Cordelia**: This is stupid. I'm your daughter. Of course I love you.
>
> **Goneril**: SOOOOOO much!
>
> **Regan**: No. SOOOOOOOOOOOOOOOOO much!!!!!!
>
> **Goneril**: !!!!!!!!!!
>
> **Regan**: !!!!!!!!!!!!!!!!!!!

Oh no! Cordelia did indeed need to give **Lear** a **Load of Crap** and **Exclamation Points** to prove she loves him! Now she's banished and sent off with the **King of France** without any inheritance!

> **The Earl of Kent**: That seems pretty unfair.

The Earl of Kent is banished too!

Goneril wrote on **Regan's Wall**.

"Wow, Dad's really losing it."

Regan wrote on **Goneril's Wall**.

"Yeah! What can we do with that?"

Gloucester can't believe the king's behavior!

> **Gloucester**: Can you believe it, my bastard son?
>
> **Edmund**: Nope. Or that your other, legitimate son is plotting against you.
>
> **Gloucester**: How dare he!
>
> **Edmund**: Thanks, gods, for standing up for this bastard.

Edmund wrote on **Edgar's Wall**.

"Hey, did you do something to piss Dad off? Maybe you should sneak around with a sword, looking like you want to kill someone."

Lear is enjoying his retirement! He gets to hang out with his men in Goneril's castle.

 Goneril sent **Lear** an **Eviction Notice**.

> **Goneril**: You have to leave unless you get rid of 50 of your flackies.

Lear at least has one daughter left! He'll go where Regan's staying and keep his men.

> **Regan**: Okay, but you can only keep 25 men.
>
> **Lear**: Okay, I'll keep 50 and go to Goneril's.
>
> **Goneril**: Maybe you could get by with 10 men? Maybe 5?
>
> **Regan**: How 'bout none?

The **Fool** says if you're such an old man, why aren't you smarter?

Regan and **Cornwall** blocked access to their account.

Lear is now running around with The Fool in the rain.

Edmund thinks Edgar needs to sign off for a while.

Edmund added "cutting my arm with daggers" to his **Activities**.

Edmund is playing **Fratricide**! If he can get his dad killed, he'll earn an **Earldom**!

Edgar updated his profile. He's now **Poor Tom**.

Edgar is ripping off his clothes, covering himself in mud, and wandering the countryside.

Lear is playing **Bring It On** with **Mother Nature**! He earned 500 points in **Being Barking Mad**.

Lear created a new **Group: King Loopy and His Freaks of Nature**. Members include **Disguised Kent**, **The Fool**, and **Naked Edgar AKA Poor Tom**.

Edgar is realizing that being Poor Tom isn't as bad as being a king who just lost his power, his daughters, and his marbles.

Edmund suggested a **Person to Torture** to **Regan** and **Cornwall**.

Gloucester can't see how this happened.

Cornwall added the **Ocular Digging** application.

Gloucester can't see.

Gloucester is realizing his bastard son is a real bastard.

Cordelia added "Leader of the French Army" to her **Work Info**.

Cordelia, **Goneril**, and **Regan** earned the highest scores ever in the game **Sibling Rivalry**.

Gloucester requested that **Poor Tom** add "The White Cliffs of Dover" to his playlist.

 Edmund, Goneril, and **Regan** all added "Bizarre Love Triangle" to their playlists.

Lear loves flowers. Flowers flowers flowers flowers. Oh, look, an army.

? **Edgar** took the quiz **If Your Dad Wanted You to Push Him Off a Cliff, Would You Do It?** with the result "No, I'd just make him think he's killing himself and then tell him I'm kidding!"

Cordelia wants to see if her father recognizes her in her new profile.

> **Lear**: I don't know where I am or how I got here. Does that make me crazy?
>
> **Cordelia**: Possibly.

 Cordelia and **Lear** are playing **Father and Child Reunion**.

 Regan shared an **Edmund** with **Goneril**.

 Edgar challenged **Edmund** to a **Duel**! Edgar beat the bastard!

 Regan, Goneril, Cornwall, Edmund, and **Gloucester** joined the group **People Who Had No Chance of Surviving Shakespeare's Most Depressing Tragedy**.

 Cordelia joined too. Then **Lear** joined.

Edgar thinks really it's a wonder they made it as long as they did.

King Lear's Fool
PROFILE

Basic Information

Networks: The Royal Court of Looneytown

Personal Information

Activities: Breaking dramatic tension while slyly driving the point of the drama home, being so ridiculous I make the crazy king look normal (though this is getting harder and harder these days)

Interests: Rhyming, mismatched clothes, my coxcomb, condescension masked as buffoonery

Wall

 The Fool can't say this to your face, so he'll say it here: You're a MORON. You're very dumb.

 The Fool thinks that was ludicrous what you did, giving your kingdom to two of your daughters and banishing the only one who ISN'T TRYING TO KILL YOU.

 The Fool also, by the way, is not enjoying being out in this rainstorm.

 The Fool is not screaming and dancing wildly to be entertaining; it's because Goneril scares the BEJEEZUS out of me, and this is how I cope.

 The Fool wonders who names their kid Goneril anyway? I know! A COMPLETE DUMBASS names their kid Goneril.

 The Fool is crying on the inside. I know. I'm such a cliché.

Oedipus Rex
NEWS FEED

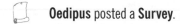 **Oedipus** posted a **Survey**.

Listen up, Thebes, and you, whiny Chorus. The Oracle of Delphi says we won't get rid of this plague till we expel the murderer of Laius, because he (she?) is in our midst. I know you didn't go after his killer when it happened because you were all about the Curse of the Sphinx then, but we've got to figure it out or we're literally doomed. So let me know:

Do you know anything about Laius's murder? *Yes No*

Have you heard your neighbors talking about anything Laius-y?
Yes No

Are you Laius's murderer? *Yes No*

 **Oedipus** wrote on **Tiresias's Wall**.

"Man, if it turns out to be someone in my family, they're going to get royally punished. Tiresias, you know about this?"

● **Tiresias** knows something you don't know.

● **Oedipus** would like Tiresias, the mean, old, stupid, blind prophet, to tell us who the murderer is.

Tiresias added the **Pleading the Fifth** application.

Oedipus created the **I'm the King and I'm Charging You with Murder If You Won't Tell Us Who the Murderer Is** application.

> **Tiresias**: Okay, it's you.
>
> **Oedipus**: Me? How dare you say that!
>
> **Tiresias**: You made me speak.
>
> **Oedipus**: Speak what?

> **Tiresias**: What.

> **Oedipus**: For Apollo's sake.

● **Oedipus** is now berating an old blind man.

● **Tiresias** says fine. Laius's killer is his children's father and brother, and his wife's husband and son.

> **Chorus**: Huh?

📷 **Oedipus** wrote on **Jocasta's Wall**.

> *"Stupid Tiresias. Thinks he knows me. He don't know me."*

● **Jocasta** is not a fan of Prophets.

> **Jocasta**: Just look at Laius! That Delphic Oracle told him he'd be murdered by his own son, and that obviously didn't happen because he was killed by thieves, and his son was cast out of town as a baby.

> **Oedipus**: Why does that sound so familiar? You know that same Oracle told ME I'd kill my father and marry my mother.

> **Jocasta**: See? That's crazy.

● **The Messenger** says Oedipus's father, Polybus, is dead, but not killed by Oedipus.

☛ **Oedipus** is **doing a jig with Jocasta! Prophesize something**, **send a Mother's Day gift**, **celebrate your Wedding Anniversary with**, or **do something else** back!

● **Oedipus** is still worried about the marrying his mother thing.

● **The Messenger** says oh, don't worry, I know Polybus and Merope aren't your actual parents, thanks to the Obviously Abandoned Baby Detector application.

> **Oedipus**: Intriguing! Tell me more.

> **Messenger**: I actually found you. You'd been cast out into the wild.

> **Jocasta**: Oh, boy.

Oedipus: No kidding! Where'd I come from?

Jocasta: Um.

Messenger: Oh, this shepherd from Laius's house gave you to me.

Jocasta is screaming at the top of her lungs and running back into the palace.

 Oedipus is working on his **Family Tree**.

 Oedipus is **solving a riddle**! He's the top-scoring riddle-solver in his kingdom.

 Oedipus is asking the Old Shepherd about Oedipus's secret identity.

> **Shepherd**: I swear you don't want to know this.
>
> **Oedipus**: What's say we torture you into telling me.
>
> **Shepherd**: The baby I gave to the messenger was Laius's child. Jocasta gave it to me to destroy because of some prophecy of the kid killing his parents someday. And that baby was you.

Oedipus has some things to talk over with the wife.

 Jocasta sent herself a **Noose**.

 Jocasta joined the group **Women Who Don't Defy Gravity**.

 Oedipus has achieved the **Highest-Ever Poking Level** by extreme-poking his own eyes out! He can finally see the truth now, just nothing else.

Oedipus is banishing himself.

Oedipus removed "genealogy" from his **Interests**.

Of Mice and Men

 George sent **Lennie** a **Cracking Egg**.

> **Lennie**: What is the egg doing, George?
>
> **George**: Just be a little patient, Lennie.
>
> **Lennie**: An egg isn't very soft, George. I can't pet an egg.
>
> **George**: Just wait a little bit, and something soft will come out of it.

● **George** is buckin' barley.

> **Lennie**: George! Will a little chick come out of the egg? And I can pet it, George? But I won't pet it too much. Is it a chick, George?
>
> **George**: Well, I wasn't fixin' to tell you this ahead of time, but a rabbit's going to hatch out of that egg after a few days.
>
> **Lennie**: Oh, George, a rabbit! Will I get to tend 'um and give 'um water an' like that?
>
> **George**: Not sure if that's part of the application, but . . .
>
> **Curley's Wife**: Any of you seen Curley?
>
> **George**: Curley ain't been here.
>
> **Lennie**: When is the egg gonna crack, George?

● **George** don't want to get mixed up in nothing. Lennie and him got to make a stake.

> **Lennie**: The egg is hatching, George! When will the rabbit be ready to pet?
>
> **George**: Maybe I shoulda told you this before, Lennie, but what I gave you, why it's not an actual egg, but . . .
>
> **Curley**: Any you guys seen my wife?
>
> **George**: She ain't been here.
>
> **Lennie**: Tell about the rabbit again, George.

● **Lennie** is smiling, thinking about livin' on the fatta the lan'. And rabbits.

> **Curley**: What the hell you laughin' at?
>
> **Lennie**: George?
>
> **Curley**: Get up on your feet, you big bastard! I'll show you who's yella!
>
> **George**: Get 'im Lennie!

● **Lennie** is pulling Curley up by the fist and crushing every bone in his hand.

 George sent **Lennie** a **Real Puppy**.

● **Lennie** is petting the puppy.

● **Lennie** would like a new puppy now.

● **Lennie** is still dreaming about the rabbits.

> **Lennie**: It's hatched, George! When can I pet the rabbit? And feed it the cut grass? And it'll nibble an' nibble the way they do?
>
> **George**: What I was tryin' to explain was this here's not a real rabbit, but a little drawing of a rabbit.

Lennie: But you promised, George! Why would I want to pet a drawing of a rabbit? If I can't feed it grass and ten' to it? Why would I want that, George?

George: I can't tell you, Lennie. I just don't know.

Lennie became a fan of **Curley's Wife's Hair**.

Lennie is petting Curley's Wife's hair.

Lennie would like a new Curley's Wife now.

Lennie remembered where to go if he jus' happened to get in trouble like he always done before.

Lennie: Go on, George, ain't you gonna give me hell?

George: Hell? Well, no. Ain't gonna give you hell. Gonna give you something though.

Lennie: Not one of those hatching eggs, George.

George: No. No hatching egg. Now why don't you look over there?

Lennie: That cracking egg, why would I want that? Can't feed the rabbit or ten' to it. Just dumb. Now a real rabbit would . . .

Death of a Salesman
NEWS FEED

- **Biff Loman** is eating dinner.

  > **Willy**: What kind of status update is that? It's got no personality!

- **Biff Loman** is pondering the point of his existence.

  > **Willy**: You've become a moody man. Who wants to know you're doing that?
  >
  > **Linda**: He's just trying to find himself, dear.
  >
  > **Willy**: Will you let me finish? Biff, just tell a joke. That's what they want to hear.

- **Biff Loman** is thinking?

  > **Willy**: Don't undersell yourself, boy. It's not what you say but how you say it!
  >
  > **Happy**: What he means to say is he's got a plan. A feasible idea.
  >
  > **Willy**: He doesn't have an idea. He's a lazy bum!
  >
  > **Linda**: No, he's not, dear.
  >
  > **Willy**: Would you let me comment?

- **Biff Loman** could use a stiff drink.

  > **Willy**: Oh, Biff. You used to be so well-liked.

- **Willy** would like to restore all of his settings to those from twenty years ago.

- **Willy** suggests Biff remove anything on his profile that's changed since That Game at Ebbets Field.

- **Willy** sent out hundreds of friend requests.

- **Willy's** only friend, Charley, makes him mad and jealous, and they kind of hate each other.

Willy added **Idealized Memories That Aren't Even That Ideal** to his **Places I'd Like to Visit Right Now**.

Willy thinks the Chevrolet is the greatest car ever built and they ought to prohibit the manufacture of that Chevrolet.

Willy is known by the finest people up and down New England, and he's lonely and people laugh at him.

Willy became a fan of **Giant Contradictions**.

Willy sent **Stockings** to **The Woman**.

Linda is mending her stockings.

Linda thinks Willy should notice that Biff is rough with the girls, steals things, drives a car without a license, and is failing math. And Happy. He should notice Happy.

> **Willy**: But Football! Adonis and Hercules!
>
> **Imaginary Brother Ben**: Diamonds! Africa!

Willy thinks Bernard isn't going to amount to anything because he isn't well-liked.

Bernard is adding "arguing a case before the Supreme Court" to his **Activities**.

Linda sent **Biff** and **Happy** a **Talking To**.

> **Linda**: Attention must be paid to such a person as your father!

Linda says Willy has been trying to erase his own profile.

Linda says Willy's life is in your hands.

Biff says oh, no pressure at all then.

Happy added the **Think Up a Useless Idea That Isn't Going to Help Anyone** application.

 Willy sent a $65-a-week request.

 Willy sent a $50-a-week request.

 Willy sent a $40-a-week request.

 Willy will now earn no dollars a week.

 Willy took the **What Kind of Fruit Are You?** quiz, with the result "I am not a piece of fruit!"

 Charley sent **Willy** a **Job Offer**.

 Willy is insulted Charley would do that and will now take Charley's money and go.

 Willy is mumbling in the street about a football.

 Willy was invited to attend **Dysfunctional Father-Son Dinner at Frank's Chop House**.

 Biff realized something about himself. Also, he stole a pen.

 Happy just wants to hit on this prostitute.

Willy was sent the **Truth** but doesn't trust that application.

Willy added **Memories of When It All Went Wrong** to his **Places I'm Mentally Visiting in This Restaurant Bathroom**.

Young Biff interrupted **Willy's** game of **Classic Midlife Crisis Affair**.

> **Young Biff**: You're a phony little fake.

Willy sent **Biff** an **Order to Take That Back**.

Willy added the **Having a Breakdown in Real Time** application.

Willy is working on his **Small Fertile Square**.

Biff and **Happy** both earned an **Even Bigger Talking To** with a possible bonus, **Expulsion from This House for the Rest of Your Lives**.

● **Biff** is trying to say good-bye to Willy.

● **Biff** likes Willy. Isn't that remarkable?

 Willy is playing "On the Road Again."

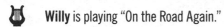 **Willy** joined the group **Men Who Shouldn't Drive at the End of a Tragedy**.

The Great Gatsby

NEWS FEED

Profile of James Gatz

Hometown: Nowheresville, North Dakota

Education Info: Two weeks at St. Olaf's

Work Info: Janitor, clam-digger

Interests: Baseball, trying to make a buck

Activities: Bettering myself, fishing

 James edited Hometown, **Education Info**, **Work Info**, **Interests**, **Activities**, and **Name** in his profile.

Profile of Jay Gatsby

Hometown: West Egg, My Yacht

Education Info: Oxford

Work Info: "Drugstore" chain owner, possible German spy, Guy Who They Say Once Killed a Man in Cold Blood

Interests: Pink suits, DAISIES

Activities: Social nihilism, bacchanals, gambling, bootlegging, fraternizing with unsavory characters, springing from a Platonic conception of myself, honing one of those rare smiles with a quality of eternal reassurance in it, staring obsessively at a green light, and creating a personal mythology for the love of a shallow married woman who I know still loves me I know it I do

Nick Carraway joined the **West Egg** network.

Nick was not aware of the famous East Egg–West Egg rivalry.

Nick is now friends with **Daisy Buchanan**, **Tom Buchanan**, and **Jordan Baker**.

Jordan is accentuating her erect carriage by throwing her body backward at the shoulders like a young cadet.

Tom joined the group **Obvious Racists**.

Daisy hopes her daughter is a beautiful little fool.

Nick added "Awful Rich People" to his **Interests**.

Nick was invited to attend **One of Gatsby's Insanely Tacky Parties**.

Gatsby wrote on **Nick's Wall**.

> *"You may not see me, as I'll be sitting on a lofty perch not drinking and watching everyone make fools of themselves. But have fun!"*

Nick met Gatsby by accident.

Nick is now an **Old Sport**.

Nick and Gatsby are attending **1920s New York City**.

Gatsby posted **Links** to his past.

Gatsby, in fact, carries around Links to his past in his pocket! Like this 100 percent genuine Montenegrin War Medal! See? A War Medal!

Nick might believe Gatsby more if he didn't say he's from that great Midwestern city, San Francisco.

Nick might think Gatsby was more honest if he didn't just introduce him to Meyer Wolfsheim, the fixer of the 1919 World Series.

Nick and **Jordan** are now "In a Lugubrious Relationship."

 Jordan is explaining that Gatsby and Daisy knew each other long ago.

 Nick thinks Jordan's story delivered Gatsby suddenly from the womb of his purposeless splendor.

 Jordan sent **Nick** a **Scornful Smile**.

 Nick is playing **Arranged Reunion**!

> *Will Daisy be happy to see Gatsby again? Or will they spend an awkward afternoon saying the wrong things and sitting around looking at each other?*

 Gatsby is playing **Rich Guy Show and Tell**.

Gatsby is running down like an over-wound clock.

Daisy is crying about expensive shirts.

Daisy has a voice with a deathless song.

 Nick added the **Third Wheel** application.

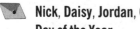 **Nick**, **Daisy**, **Jordan**, **Gatsby**, and **Tom** are attending **Terrible Luncheon on the Hottest Day of the Year**.

Daisy is speaking in an indiscreet voice full of money.

Gatsby sent **Everyone** a **Facial Expression at Once Definitely Unfamiliar and Vaguely Recognizable**.

Tom is feeling the hot whips of panic.

Nick is just feeling hot.

Tom and **Gatsby** are playing **Upper-Crust Pissing Match**! They're being passive-aggressive, getting worked up in fancy hotels, and tooling around in each other's cars.

● **Gatsby** is trying to touch what is no longer tangible, struggling unhappily, undespairingly, toward that lost voice across the room.

● **Nick** just realized it's his birthday.

> **Tom**: Your birthday! Why didn't you tell us? Happy B-day, man!
>
> **Jordan**: Have a great one! Hope you do something fun!
>
> **Gatsby**: You're old, Old Sport! LOL.
>
> **Oedipus**: What? A birthday? And you probably know who your mother is. Good for you.
>
> **Frankenstein's Monster**: And you probably HAD a mother, which is good too.
>
> **William Shakespeare**: Happy Birthday to you! Happy Birthday to you!
>
> **Oscar Wilde**: Cheers on your birthday!
>
> **Ernest Hemingway**: Drinks are on me and Scottie! Ignore that Zelda.
>
> **Anna Karenina**: Sending you birthday love across the networks! Have a wonderful time!
>
> **Daisy**: How wonderful, Nick. Have a beautiful day. Do something fun!
>
> **Nick**: Thanks for the wishes, all you people I don't know, but I spent it with a bunch of jerks at the Plaza watching Tom and Gatsby threaten to kill each other. It's actually been quite miserable.
>
> **Tom**: Have a blast!

● **Gatsby** and **Daisy**, and **Tom**, **Jordan**, and **Nick** are driving toward death through the cooling twilight.

● **Myrtle Wilson** is trying to stop Gatsby's car with Myrtle Wilson.

 Daisy and **Gatsby** lost a round of **Hit and Run**.

● **Gatsby** is outside Daisy's house watching over nothing.

🎀 **Wilson** received a **message** from the **Eyes of God (or possibly an old billboard)**.

- **Wilson** thinks he knows who killed his wife.

- **Gatsby** is taking a dip in the pool!

 **Gatsby** joined the group **Men Who Float But Are Still Not Impervious to Bullets**.

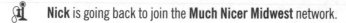 **Nick** is going back to join the **Much Nicer Midwest** network.

- **Tom** and **Daisy** added **Back into Our Vast Carelessness** to their **Places I'm Going to Visit**.

? **Nick** took the quiz **What If You Had a Funeral and Nobody Came?**

- **Nick** is thinking of the first explorers.

- **Nick** is thinking about the green light.

- **F. Scott Fitzgerald** became a fan of **Fairly Obvious But Eloquently Written Metaphors**.

- **Nick** is thinking about how we'll keep fighting the current to go forward even if it just keeps pushing us back.

Fan Page

Dr. T. J. Eckleburg's Optical Emporium

Become a fan!

Information: Eckleburg's Optical Emporium has a SPEC-tacular variety of glasses and frames to light up the peepers of every flapper and dapper! So get on your glad rags, and get an EYE-full at our g-EYE-ant showroom in beautiful Astoria, Queens.

Look for our billboard in the lovely stretch of land between the City and the Eggs!

Wall

Owl Eyes wrote
Love your work, Eckleburg! Always a stand-up selection of swell specs that help me live up to my name!

Wilson wrote
God?

Nick Carraway wrote
If you don't mind my saying so, I believe your billboard in the Valley of Ashes is ready for a new paint job. People here have taken it to be a giant symbol of a higher being watching over them and their misdeeds.

F. Scott Fitzgerald wrote
Shhh!

Nick Carraway wrote
It broods over the solemn dumping ground, this fantastic farm where ashes grow like wheat into ridges and hills and grotesque gardens. And creeps me out on the train.

Owl Eyes wrote
Another fine choice, Eckleburg! These specs should help when I'm trying to drive home so blotto I don't notice when a wheel's dropped off the car.

Wilson wrote
God?

Wilson wrote
Is that you?

The House of Mirth

NEWS FEED

 Lily Bart became a fan of **Gambling**.

> **Lily**: No, I meant Cambling. It's a new game. All the rage.

 Lily would really rather not play Bridge for money.

 Lily will bet you how long it will take for you to convince her to join the Bridge game.

 Lily is listed as "Single."

 Lily is donating her status to request an update to her status.

 Lily invited you to join her **Cause**.

> *"Support my cause, The Lily Bart Fund, by donating to it, investing in it, or, preferably, being wealthy and asking me to marry you."*

 Lily and **Lawrence Selden** are now friends.

Lily received a **Marriage Proposal** from **Selden**.

> **Lily**: But how many friends do you have? And who are they?
>
> **Lily**: And how big is your Small Fertile Square?
>
> **Lily**: And what level of poking have you achieved?
>
> **Lily**: And what kind of Vampire are you?
>
> **Lily**: And what's your highest WordJumble score?
>
> **Lily**: And how many cities have you visited?
>
> **Lily**: And what groups are you in?

 Selden sent **Lily** an **Okay, Let's Be Friends Who Crush on One Another** request.

The What a Piece of Work Network Quiz:

Are You a Good Son or Daughter?

Your parents surely love you. But how do you treat *them*? Put these in the order of things you are **MOST** to **LEAST** likely to do.

—Send a Mother's Day card.
—Call your parents once a week to talk about what's going on in your life.
—Change your name, leave home, and pretend you came from somewhere else.
—Fail to live up to your father's inflated expectations.
—Leave your father talking to himself in a restaurant bathroom.
—Lock your father out of your house in a horrific rainstorm.
—Trick your father into thinking his other son is trying to kill him.
—Plot revenge against your mother's new husband.
—Flatter your father to his face, then do everything you can to drive him insane.
—Stab your father to death, marry your mother, drive her to suicide, and pierce out both your eyes.

Lily is impressed by the amount of things in Percy Gryce's profile.

Percy Gryce added the **Bellomont Summer Home** to **Places I'm Visiting to See Lily Bart**.

Lily is attending a **Walk with Her Friend-He's-Just-a-Friend Lawrence Selden**.

Bertha Dorset posted a **Link**: **Lily Bart's Infamous Closet Skeletons**.

Percy Gryce has signed out of the **Bellomont Summer Home**.

Lily keeps hearing about this stock market thing.

Lily sent an **Investment** request to **Gus Trenor**.

> **Gus**: Why sure, pretty lady, I'll do that for you. It'll be our little secret.

Lily sent **Gus** a **Wary Smile**.

Lily is on top of the world!

Lily is totally miserable.

Lily is so much better than so many people!

Lily is just the lowest of the low.

Lily's going to marry well and rise to the top of New York society!

Lily's going to die penniless and alone in a dingy little dung hole.

Lily received a vicious bout of **Status Update Fluctuitis**.

Gus sent **Lily** a **Why Don't You Ever Talk to Me?** demand.

> **Lily**: Where's your wife?

Gus has been playing **Bilk Her**! He took **Lily's** money, didn't invest it, and just sent her checks of his own. Now she owes him thousands of dollars! But he'll easily forget that if she just gives him the sex.

 Lily sent **Gus** a **Huffy Door Slam**.

 Lily added **The Brink of Poverty** to her **Places I've Visited**.

 Lily received a **Marriage Proposal** from **Simon Rosedale**.

> **Lily**: But do you have an Ocean Reef?
>
> **Lily**: And what movies do you like? Are we compatible?
>
> **Lily**: And what quizzes have you taken?
>
> **Lily**: And what's your true age?
>
> **Lily**: And have you Elfed yourself? Or put your head on a cartoon body? Or your face on someone else's head? Because that could expel us from high society.

 Rosedale will just wait here while Lily makes up her mind.

 Lily is attending **Bertha's Mediterranean Cruise Where She Can Distract Everyone from the Affair Bertha's Having**.

 Lily forgot to distract everyone from the affair Bertha's having.

 Lily is being expelled from society (and Bertha's yacht).

 Lily received a **Snub** from her **Aunt's Last Will and Testament**.

 Lily received a **Help Refusal** from her cousin **Grace**.

Lily received a **You Missed Your Chance** notice from **Simon Rosedale**.

Lily received a **Who Are You Again?** notice from **Gus and Judy Trenor**.

Lily received a **Well What Do You Want Me to Do?** shrug from **Selden**.

Lily is adding some "Actual Work Info" to her **Work Info**.

 Lily updated her profile. She's now **Working-Class Lily**.

 Lily joined the group **Former High-Society Women Ill-Equipped to Make Hats**.

 Lily became a fan of **Sleep Medication**.

 Lily is visiting Lawrence Selden.

> **Selden**: Aren't you going to ask me about my number of friends?
>
> **Selden**: Or my Small Fertile Square?
>
> **Selden**: Or my poking ability?
>
> **Selden**: Or my Vampire?
>
> **Lily**: No. I'm just going to cry and be really honest.
>
> **Selden**: How novel! I don't think I'm prepared to show any kind of emotion, so I'll just stand here and worry about you but do nothing.

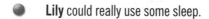

 Lily received **A Check to Pay Off All the Debt**.

 Lily could really use some sleep.

Lily added the **Sleep** application. Then added a little more of the **Sleep** application. And a little more of the **Sleep** application.

 Selden is finally ready to change his **Relationship Status** with **Lily**!

Selden received **Edith Wharton's Tragic Twist on a Novel of Manners Ending**.

Selden sent **Lily** an **Ironic, Sad, and Long-Overdue Hug**.

The What a Piece of Work Network Plays Scrabulific!

	B		
	O		
	R		
S	I	G	H
	N		A
	G		T

SMACK TALK!

Daisy Buchanan: Hat! Ha ha! Hat! How quaint and lovely of you to play *hat*.

Jordan Baker: I think it's quite ridiculous, actually.

Lily Bart: I'm sorry. I just didn't have many letters left after pawning them for a new set of monogrammed handkerchiefs, and *hat* is the best I could do.

Jordan: Blah blah blah hat. That's all I heard.

Daisy: I think *hat* is a fine word. It's a romantic word, isn't it? Doesn't she remind you of a rose? An absolute rose?

Jordan: More like a dandelion in a windstorm.

Holden Caulfield: Aw, I can't stand you phonies. I swear to God.

Jordan: How did THAT get in here?

Daisy: Why, it's a young man with a perky little hunting cap! How divine!

Holden: I'm not divine. I'm a madman. And I think her word *hat* is swell.

Jordan: Swell. Swell. Look at it speak.

Lily: Thank you, sir, but I can't possibly repay you for defending me. I also can't be seen commenting with you in good society.

Holden: I'm actually loaded with cash. But I wouldn't want to ruin your crumby game by embarrassing you in front of your "friends."

Jordan: Ha. Friends. Ha. I'm laughing my ass off. Oh.

Lily: I do apologize. Please wait. Oh, he's gone. Where'd he go? Please come back.

Jordan: Let's go, Daisy. We'll put little white dresses on, make a pitcher of something clinky, and pretend we're going to play tennis.

Daisy: Oh, yes, let's. God, we're sophisticated.

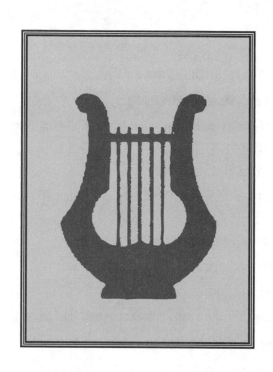

8

Estragon dedicated "Should I Stay or Should I Go" to Vladimir.

The Wordplay Network

Cymbeline • Jack Kerouac • William Faulkner • Mrs. Dalloway • James Joyce • Slaughterhouse-Five • Waiting for Godot

Cymbeline

 Imogen is now married to **Posthumus**.

> **Cymbeline**: I thought this was a comedy. Don't the comedies usually END in weddings? Plus, I didn't want my daughter Imogen to marry that guy.
>
> **Cloten**: I thought I was supposed to marry her.
>
> **Cymbeline**: What kind of name is that anyway? Posthumus.

 Cymbeline sent a **Banishment** to **Posthumus**.

 Cymbeline sent **Imogen** to prison.

> **Imogen**: So this is kind of King Lear-y then? A tragedy?
>
> **Posthumus**: There are prisons in the comedies though. Maybe it's a romance?
>
> **Imogen**: Shakespeare did romances?
>
> **Posthumus**: Troilus and Cressida. Antony and Cleopatra.
>
> **Imogen**: Never heard of 'em.

● **The Queen** is not your typical stepmother.

> **The Queen**: I just rule over my husband and undermine everyone for my own spiteful gain.
>
> **Posthumus**: Oh, like Lady Macbeth.
>
> **Imogen**: It IS a tragedy.

● **Cloten's Henchmen** are making all kinds of penis puns.

> **Imogen**: Comedy!

> **Cymbeline**: Yes, comedy.
>
> **Posthumus**: Tragicomedy?

Posthumus added **Rome** to his **Cities I've Visited**.

> **Imogen**: We were in Roman Empire—era Britain, and now he's in Renaissance Italy?
>
> **Posthumus**: I'm so confused.

Iachimo challenged **Posthumus** to a **Bet**. **Imogen**, like any stupid woman, will be seduced by his charms or he owes **Posthumus** 10,000 ducats.

> **Posthumus**: Comedy! Though I don't find this arc funny at all.

The Queen became a fan of **Poison**.

Cornelius thinks she's sketchy and is subbing out the Poison she wanted for Deathlike-Sleeping Potion.

> **Cloten**: OOH! OOH! Romeo and Juliet!
>
> **Posthumus**: Why is Shakespeare ripping himself off like that?
>
> **Imogen**: Maybe that's why we're called a "problem play."
>
> **James Joyce**: Maybe he's just tired of conforming to expectations.
>
> **Samuel Beckett**: Maybe he wants to leave it open to interpretation.
>
> **William Faulkner**: Maybe he's drunk.

Iachimo sent a **Lustful Hug** to **Imogen**.

Imogen will not open any of Iachimo's requests.

Iachimo is sneaking into Imogen's bedchamber in a trunk, taking note of the room furnishings, looking at Imogen's birthmark, and stealing a bracelet.

> **Cymbeline**: See? Comedy. If he was a true tragic villain, he wouldn't deign to sneak into a room in a trunk.

Iago: A true villain would have talked her into that Lustful Hug with his cunning language.

Richard III: A true villain would have married her already and be plotting how to kill her in order to marry someone else and advance his power.

Iago: And a true villain wouldn't have just stolen a bracelet out of her bedchamber, if you know what I'm saying.

Richard III: Touché.

● **Iachimo** is back in Italy.

> **Posthumus**: Wow, you got here quick.
>
> **Iachimo**: Yeah! Especially since we seem to be in different time periods.
>
> **Billy Pilgrim**: What's wrong with that?

● **Iachimo** is falsifying the results of the Bet.

✉ **Posthumus** sent a **Murder My Cheating Wife** request to his servant **Pisanio**.

> **Cymbeline**: Othello!

● **Pisanio** is ignoring the request and convincing Imogen to dress as a boy and find her husband.

> **Imogen**: Twelfth Night?

 Pisanio sent a **Fake Murder Completed** message to **Posthumus**.

> **Cymbeline**: Much Ado About Nothing, I think. This is fun. Keep going.

 Imogen added "spelunking" to her **Interests**.

> **Imogen**: Okay, I'm totally lost. I'm supposed to find my long-lost brothers in this cave? This is crazy. How can you add main characters in the third act?
>
> **James Joyce**: I'm following it all swimmingly.

Kurt Vonnegut: Me too.

William Faulkner: Ditto.

Imogen: Where am I? Wales now? Am I still dressed like a boy?

The Queen: Am I even still in this play anymore?

 Cloten challenged **Guiderius** to a **Duel**. Congratulations, **Guiderius**! You move on to the next round.

Kurt Vonnegut: So it goes.

Cloten: What??? I'm dead? Who's Guiderius?

The Queen sent **Sleep Medicine** to **Imogen**.

Guiderius: Oh no, she's dead!

Kurt Vonnegut: So it goes.

Friar Lawrence: No, not dead! Looks dead, but not dead.

Imogen: It's okay, I woke up and thought dead Cloten was dead Posthumus, and it looks like I'm working for the Roman army now.

Billy Pilgrim: I can relate.

Posthumus is dressing in disguise and fighting in some kind of battle?

James Joyce: Don't worry, getting through what some may call a "dense" story always pays off in the end.

William Faulkner: It's true.

The God Jupiter: I'm told I'm supposed to have a walk-on here?

Imogen: This is ridiculous. You don't even sound like a Shakespeare character.

James Joyce: He's playing with the form! Who said literature was supposed to be easy? It's a pastiche, a pastiche of his earlier plays and of language.

Cymbeline: Are we totally sure Shakespeare even wrote this play?

Virginia Woolf: Maybe it was his sister.

Cloten: This is a terrible play. I'd like to post a complaint.

Imogen: I don't think you can do that on a news feed. You need a group page or something.

Posthumus: Or a fan page?

Cymbeline: My head hurts.

● **Cymbeline** would like someone to clear up all this confusion.

Cornelius: First off, the Queen is dead, she never loved you, and she was planning on killing you anyway.

Kurt Vonnegut: So it goes.

Imogen: I, a Roman page boy, would like to know why Iachimo is wearing Posthumus's ring.

Iachimo: Sorry, it was this stupid bet. And I kind of got Posthumus to think Imogen cheated on him so he ordered to have her killed.

Posthumus: I should kill YOU!

Imogen: Hey, you guys, it's me, Imogen!

Posthumus: Ohhhhh. Hi, babe.

Guiderius: And me and my brother are Cymbeline's long-lost sons.

Soothsayer: And Zeus prophesized all of this.

Cymbeline: Cool. So I should just free these Romans and forget about why we had a war in the first place?

Imogen: Sounds good.

Cymbeline invited **Everyone** to attend a **Play-Ending Feast**.

> **James Joyce**: I told you it would make sense in the end. Sometimes it's good to hear a story that isn't easily categorized.
>
> **Jack Kerouac**: Yes, but to truly break the mold, his sentences could have been longer.
>
> **Virginia Woolf**: Or he could have more parentheticals and semicolons.
>
> **William Faulkner**: Or maybe just not bother to tell you who's speaking or use punctuation. Or put Act III, Scene II, at the start of Act I.
>
> **Jack Kerouac**: Or make the sentences more like jazz.
>
> **Virginia Woolf**: Or waves.
>
> **Samuel Beckett**: Or use more religious metaphors.
>
> **James Joyce**: And he really could lose the whole Jupiter character.
>
> **The God Jupiter**: Why pick on me? I don't even know where I am or WHO I am or what it all means. What does it all mean?
>
> **James Joyce**: Exactly.

PROFILE

Basic Information

Network: America

Religious Views: Buddhism, Friend Worship

Personal Information

Activities: Writing what I want bottomless from bottom of the mind, trying not to get drunk outside my own house, believing in the holy contour of life, keeping track of every day the date emblazoned in my morning

Interests: Jazz, spontaneity, the road, being the crazy dumbsaint of the mind, stream of consciousness, to pursue my star further, the mad people

Looking for: Movement, this great continent, the girl I love

Wall

Jack Kerouac is now friends with **Neal Cassady**.

> **Jack Kerouac**: My first impression of Neal was of a young Gene Autry—trim, thin-hipped, blue-eyed, with a real Oklahoma accent—a sideburned hero of the snowy west.
>
> **Neal Cassady**: Well, thanks, Jack.
>
> **Jack Kerouac**: To Neal sex was the one and only holy and important thing in life.
>
> **Neal Cassady**: I wouldn't say the ONLY important thing.

> **Jack Kerouac**: He's the holy con-man with the shining mind. And his "criminality" isn't something that sulks and sneers; it's a wild yea-saying overburst of American joy.
>
> **Neal Cassady**: Okay.
>
> **Jack Kerouac**: It's Western, the west wind, an ode from the Plains, something new, long prophesied, long a-coming.

Jack Kerouac is attending the **Denver Bar with All the Gang Tonight**, hoping that in their eyes he'll be strange and ragged and like the prophet who has walked across the land to bring the dark Word and the only word he has is "Wow!"

Jack Kerouac is now friends with **Allen Ginsberg**.

> **Jack Kerouac**: The sorrowful poetic con-man with the dark mind.
>
> **Allen Ginsberg**: Hmm.

Jack Kerouac is telling his soul whooee.

Jack Kerouac commented on his own photo in the album **Frisco**.

> *"In another hour the fog will stream through the Golden Gate to shroud the romantic city in white."*

Jack's Aunt commented on a photo in the album **Frisco**.

> *"Are you getting a job anytime soon?"*

Jack Kerouac is wearing the silliest shoes in America.

Jack Kerouac is now friends with **Henri Cru**.

> **Jack Kerouac**: Henri's just like a little boy. Somewhere in his past, in his lonely schooldays in France, they'd taken everything from him.
>
> **Henri Cru**: What?
>
> **Jack Kerouac**: He was browbeaten and thrown out of one school after another. He was out to get everything he'd lost; there was no end to his loss; this thing would drag on forever.
>
> **Henri Cru**: I really don't know where you get this stuff.

Jack Kerouac is at the midget auto races.

 Jack Kerouac is now friends with **William S. Burroughs**.

> **Jack Kerouac**: He's a teacher, and he has a sentimental streak about the old days in America when you could get morphine in drugstores without prescription.
>
> **William S. Burroughs**: Ha ha, that's so me.

 Jack Kerouac will now write status updates to the rhythm of jazz.

 Jack Kerouac began to iron a shirt; a smile broke over his ecstatic face; he began to iron in the laundry room, back and forth, slowly at first, then the steam came up, and he began ironing fast, his left foot jumped up with every hiss, his neck began to bounce crookedly, he brought his face down to the shirt, he pushed his hair back, his combed hair dissolved, he began to sweat.

 Jack Kerouac was invited to attend **New York with Neal Cassady**.

> **Jack Kerouac**: Be right with you.

 Jack Kerouac felt the heat pick up. He hunched over and soaked it in, faster and faster, it seemed faster and faster, that's all. He began to work the collar; it rolled under the iron in great rich mist, you'd think he wouldn't have time to line it up. The cotton rolled and rolled like the sea.

 Neal Cassady wrote

> *Now Jack, we've got thirty hours to go a thousand miles.*

 Jack Kerouac, he was done. On the board the iron sat; its silver shadow made a strange reflection on the washing machine behind the pile of mismatched socks. It was a rainy night. It was the myth of a rainy night. And before him was the great bulge and bulk of his dirty clothes, the odor rising, just as it did yesterday and would tomorrow, here and in any laundry room in America.

Yoknapatawpha County

FAN PAGE

Become a fan!

Fans:

Caddy Compson, Cash Bundren, Colonel Sartoris

Information:

What: A county of northern Mississippi made famous by Mr. William Faulkner

County Seat: Jefferson

Size: 2,400 square miles of not a whole helluva lot

Current Weather: Humid with a chance of bitterness and soul-sucking

Discussion Board

Topic: Why No Love for the County?

Colonel Sartoris wrote
I don't understand why our lovely county has only three fans! In my day it was the epitome of grandeur, a place where you could be looked at as a hero even after getting kicked out of the Confederate army and shooting a couple of carpetbaggers in broad daylight.

Caddy Compson wrote
Weren't you actually shot and killed in broad daylight by some disgruntled business partner or something?

Colonel Sartoris wrote

True, true. But what an exciting and adventurous place! Why wouldn't people want to visit?

Cash Bundren wrote

Do you think it could have anything to do with Mr. Faulkner making us look like all we're interested in here is death, the fall of the South, loss of innocence, racism, being haunted by the past, burial, funerals, alcohol, the power of time, poor parenting skills . . .

Caddy Compson wrote

Arson, unwanted pregnancy, insanity, drilling holes into a coffin lid and inadvertently drilling into your dead mother's face, murder, sadism, sin, hypochondria . . .

Cash Bundren wrote

What's your story, Caddy? I know it's somewhere in that "Sound and Fury" book, but when I tried reading that, I could actually feel different parts of my brain start to pummel each other.

Caddy Compson wrote

I know. It doesn't help that whenever I'm mentioned in the book it's in disjointed flashbacks and italics with little to no punctuation.

Quentin Compson wrote

clothes upon the bed by the nose seen above the apple what he said? just seventeen, mind.

Caddy Compson wrote

See, like that. Hey Quentin, why aren't you a fan of Yoknapatawpha County?

Quentin Compson wrote

Oh Caddy Im crying how could you sister and your muddy drawers Caddy Caddy *Caddy*

Caddy Compson wrote

Oy. He's not going to be a fan of anything anytime soon.

Colonel Sartoris wrote

Indeed! These funny words aren't doing anything helpful for our tourism industry.

Flannery O'Connor wrote

William Faulkner is a giant of a writer! He's influenced so many of us with his stream-of-consciousness style and by challenging conventional literary rules.

Truman Capote wrote

I agree!

Toni Morrison wrote

Yes!

Jack Kerouac wrote
It's true!

William Shakespeare wrote
I just like his titles.

Colonel Sartoris wrote
But does that make any of you want to come down here and taste our sarsaparilla or see our community gardens that have been completely neglected due to our citizens' obsession with their rapidly dissolving family honor and inability to support any living thing?

Colonel Sartoris wrote
Anyone?

Colonel Sartoris wrote
Please?

Vardaman Bundren wrote
My mother is a fish.

Cash Bundren wrote
Um.

Colonel Sartoris wrote
Yeah, we've got a problem.

William Faulkner

PROFILE

Basic Information

Location: Rowan Oak, of course

Birthday: September 25, 1897

Groups

Member of:

Some of My Ancestors Were Killed in Duels, Nobel Laureates Who Didn't Go to College, Oxford Men, Yes I Wrote It That Way Just to Mess with You, Chronological Order Is for Sissies, SAVE WATER . . . Drink Whiskey, Important Southern Writers

Wall

 William Faulkner will write status updates for money.

 William Faulkner doesn't know how that u got in his name and doesn't much care.

 William Faulkner will write an appendix to all of this in a few decades to help it all fall into place.

 William Faulkner may or may not have a metal plate in his head.

Mrs. Dalloway

NEWS FEED

 **Clarissa Dalloway** posted an **Event**: **My Party**.

Clarissa does not need anyone to get the Flowers (Clarissa is greeting Hugh Whitbread); she will get them herself.

Clarissa received a **Reminder** of when she received a proposal from **Peter Walsh**.

Clarissa is now married to **Mr. Dalloway**.

Clarissa added "Fear no more the heat o' the sun" to her **Favorite Quotations**.

Clarissa heard a car backfire, which was also heard by . . .

Septimus Warren Smith is not a fan of that noise because he was in the war.

Septimus posted a news story.

> *The world is threatening to burst into flames.*

Septimus is looking at the car, which is also being looked at by . . .

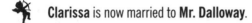 **Lucrezia Smith** is sending a silent **Stop Acting Crazy** request to her husband.

Lucrezia is watching a plane writing something in the sky, also being studied by . . .

Masie Johnson is thinking what an odd-looking couple (how frightening London is).

Masie is adding **Regent's Park** to her **Places I've Been**, as has . . .

Mrs. Dempster is thinking it's been a hard life and she could use a little pity.

Clarissa received a **Reminder** of **Sally Seton**.

Clarissa remembers the night she wore the white frock and thought of Othello's line, "if it were now to die 'twere to be most happy" and saw Sally, and then came the most exquisite moment of her life; Sally kissed her on the lips, and she uncovered the revelation, the religious feeling!—and then like running one's face against granite . . .

 Peter added the **Sweet-Moment Interrupter** application.

Real-Time Peter is at the door.

 Clarissa sent a **Kiss** to **Peter**, and all in a clap it came over her if she had married him this gaiety would be hers all day, and **Peter** is asking if she's happy in her marriage and . . .

Elizabeth (her daughter) is coming in the door asking how d'y do?

 Peter long ago removed "loving Clarissa" from his **Interests**.

Peter is in love with Daisy, and no one's in love as much as he is. Not with Clarissa.

Peter is watching a little girl run straight into the legs of . . .

Lucrezia received a **Terrified Look** from . . .

Septimus is thinking his dead friend is coming near him, but really it's . . .

Peter is thinking oh look, a young couple having a squabble.

Septimus does not want to add children to his network.

Dr. Holmes thinks Septimus is just in a funk.

Septimus is thinking Dr. Holmes is Human Nature.

 Dr. Holmes sent **Septimus** a **Get a Second Opinion** request.

Septimus is now a patient of **Sir William Bradshaw**, psychiatrist.

Septimus thinks Sir William Bradshaw is more awful than Dr. Holmes.

Richard Dalloway is thinking he should tell Clarissa he loves her. Yes, he would say that.

Richard is bearing his flowers for Clarissa like a weapon.

- **Richard** is hearing Big Ben, whose sound is flooding the drawing room of . . .

 Clarissa was given **Lovely Flowers** from . . .

 Richard is having trouble adding the **Tell Your Wife You Love Her** application.

- **Clarissa** is thinking about how one should see the sky; walk in the park; then suddenly in came Peter; then these roses—that it must end; and no one in the whole world would know.

- **Elizabeth** is standing by the door, outside of which is . . .

- **Miss Kilman** had been cheated. Didn't she have a right to happiness?

- **Miss Kilman** is wondering if she's being laughed at by . . .

 Clarissa is not a fan of **Miss Kilman**.

 Septimus added Shakespeare's words, "Fear no more," to his **Favorite Quotations**.

- **Septimus** is actually smiling, as seen by . . .

- **Lucrezia** is making a hat, and wait, is Septimus actually noticing and making her laugh?

- **Lucrezia** has never felt so happy! Never in her life! And now she's sewing as watched by . . .

- **Septimus** became himself just then.

- **Septimus** was sent a **Nightmare**.

- **Dr. Holmes** picked a really bad time to attend the **Septimus Smith Household**.

- **Dr. Holmes** is coming up the stairs as heard by . . .

- **Septimus** is deciding between the bread knife, the gas fire, and razors.

- **Septimus** is thinking this is their idea of a tragedy, not his or Lucrezia's.

- **Septimus** chose the window.

- **Peter** is hearing the ambulance and thinking what a triumph of civilization.

Clarissa sent the **Same Greeting** to **Everyone**.

● **Clarissa** hopes the party isn't a complete failure.

● **Clarissa** sees Sally Seton and is kindling all over with pleasure at the thought of the past.

● **Clarissa** wishes she didn't feel so judged by . . .

● **Peter** thanks God he doesn't live in this pernicious hubble-bubble like . . .

Clarissa is now friends with **The Prime Minister**.

 Lady Bradshaw sent **Clarissa** a **message**.

A young man has killed himself.

● **Clarissa** is thinking somehow it was her disaster—her disgrace.

● **Clarissa** is thinking fear no more the heat o' the sun.

● **Clarissa** knows she must go find people like Sally and . . .

● **Peter** is wondering where Clarissa is, as is

● **Sally** is feeling simply this. How could Clarissa have married Richard?

● **Sally** thinks Clarissa didn't care as much for Richard as she cared for . . .

● **Peter** is wondering what is this terror? This ecstasy? The thing that fills me with extraordinary excitement is . . .

● **Clarissa,** for there she is.

Virginia Woolf
PROFILE

Basic Information

Networks: England

Relationship Status:
Married to Leonard, etc.

Personal Information

Activities:
Writing, discussing writing, writing about writing, Ladies' Nights

Wall

 Virginia Woolf created the group **Bloomsbury**.

 Virginia Woolf became a fan of **Owning a Room**.

 Virginia Woolf likes **Nicole Kidman**, but was the fake nose really necessary?

 Virginia Woolf is afraid of **Edward Albee**.

James Joyce
PROFILE

Basic Information

Networks: Trieste, Zurich, Paris, The Dublin in My Mind

Birthday: February 2, 1882

Political Views: Expatriate-y

Religious Views: Don't Get Me Started

Pages: Bloomsday, *The Producers*

Wall

 James Joyce will write a status update for each hour of the day.

> **Virginia Woolf**: How novel!
>
> **William Faulkner**: Very cool.
>
> **Charles Dickens**: Why?

 James Joyce is.

> **Mark Twain**: Is . . . what?
>
> **Charles Dickens**: Yes, why not finish your sentence? You have to think about your readers. What will they make of this?
>
> **William Faulkner**: He's breaking boundaries with his status updates. He's flouting conventional wisdom!

Jane Austen: Are you sure he didn't just hit "Post" too soon?

 James Joyce Clapclap. Clipclap. Clappyclap. Big Benben. Fff! Oo!

Charles Dickens: I see, you're in London! Welcome.

William Faulkner: I don't think he's in London. I think he's using language to represent . . . train noise?

Virginia Woolf: The ticking of a clock?

James Joyce: It's music! I'm writing words to sound like music.

Jack Kerouac: Nice.

 James Joyce is THOSE SLIGHTLY RAMBUNCTIOUS FEMALES.

Nathaniel Hawthorne: You know it.

Louisa May Alcott: Nate, do you even know what he's talking about?

Nathaniel Hawthorne: I recognize some of the words.

James Joyce: It's a headline! I'm in a newspaper office, so I'm writing in the form of a headline.

Jane Austen: I don't get it.

William Faulkner: You're demonstrating how words are all around us all the time. Right?

James Joyce: Something like that.

Charles Dickens: Why?

 James Joyce would like to use this status update to discuss his theory that Shakespeare wrote Hamlet about his philandering wife.

William Shakespeare: Why bring my personal life into this?

James Joyce: Because YOU did. You were writing about your life. And your writing affects all of our writing. And art can be personal. So I'm bringing your personal art into my art.

William Shakespeare: Weird.

James Joyce: And you represented yourself with Hamlet's father, not Hamlet. Right?

William Shakespeare: Not really. There was this kid down the street whose uncle killed his dad and then married his mother. And then he would not SHUT UP about it.

James Joyce: Oh.

William Shakespeare: And he was really mean to his girlfriend.

William Shakespeare: And he was always talking about killing himself but not doing it.

William Shakespeare: And then he got killed by his girlfriend's brother.

James Joyce: I see.

William Shakespeare: And their house was haunted.

James Joyce: Right.

William Shakespeare: And they were all from Denmark.

James Joyce: Maybe I'll try writing another status update now.

William Shakespeare: And their name was the Hamlets.

James Joyce will use status updates to explore the history of the English language, starting with Latin and old Anglo-Saxon poetry and ending in American ad-speak.

 Unknown Beowulf Author likes this.

Mark Twain: Now this I can sort of understand.

Emily Brontë: Yes, he'll just write the words to mimic accents or different forms of grammar.

J. D. Salinger: Makes sense.

James Joyce: At the same time, I'd like to use language to represent the forty weeks of human gestation, and when I'm finished, a baby will be born in my status update.

Emily Brontë: Oh. Hmm. Well.

Charles Dickens: How are you enjoying London?

James Joyce (to Private Compton) **I don't know your name, but you are quite right**.

> **William Faulkner**: Ingenious. It's written like a play!
>
> **Nathaniel Hawthorne**: But who's Private Compton?
>
> **Samuel Beckett**: It doesn't matter. You'll just get a feeling of what's going on from the words without them being so precise.
>
> **William Shakespeare**: But how does a character know when to enter or exit?
>
> **Samuel Beckett**: Interesting. Maybe the characters just won't exit.
>
> **Nathaniel Hawthorne**: OR maybe he could just write like a normal person.
>
> **Nathaniel Hawthorne**: Sorry, his status updates are making me dizzy.
>
> **William Faulkner**: Why don't you steady your nerves with a drink?
>
> **James Joyce**: Yes, why not?
>
> **Ernest Hemingway**: I'll send you over a Cuba Libre right now.
>
> **Jack Kerouac**: Good idea.

 James Joyce is defecating.

> **Jane Austen**: Ewwwwwwww!
>
> **Mark Twain**: Icky.
>
> **Emily Brontë**: How absurd!
>
> **Ernest Hemingway**: Goddamn.
>
> **James Joyce**: I'm not REALLY defecating right now. It's just, how often have you seen that in a status update? Never. It really threatens your preconceived notions of what a status update should be.
>
> **William Shakespeare**: Couldn't you just couch it in some vague innuendo?
>
> **Nathaniel Hawthorne**: Couldn't you just, you know, not write that?
>
> **William Faulkner**: DRINK.

> **Jack Kerouac**: Yes, yes, yes.
>
> **Edgar Allan Poe**: Come on.
>
> **Ernest Hemingway**: Chug! Chug! Chug! Chug!
>
> **Nathaniel Hawthorne**: Serious peer pressure, people.
>
> **Emily Brontë**: Chug!
>
> **Emily Brontë**: NOW who's challenging your preconceived notions?
>
> **Emily Brontë**: Modernist, my ass.

 James Joyce wonders, was it there?

> **James Joyce**: It was in the corresponding pocket of the trousers which he had worn on the day but one preceding.
>
> **James Joyce**: Get it? It's in the form of a catechism!
>
> **William Faulkner**: Ah! Well done.
>
> **Virginia Woolf**: Fascinating.
>
> **Samuel Beckett**: Way to go.
>
> **Jack Kerouac**: Cool.
>
> **Charles Dickens**: Why?
>
> **James Joyce**: For f's sake. I guess my next book will be in a language that looks like English, but is really just crazy-talk. How about that?
>
> **Charles Dickens**: Okay.
>
> **Nathaniel Hawthorne**: I'm drunk!
>
> **William Faulkner**: Ah! Well done.
>
> **Jack Kerouac**: Cool.
>
> **James Joyce**: Way to go.

Charles Dickens wrote

But why?

Slaughterhouse-Five

NEWS FEED

● **Billy Pilgrim** is on the planet Tralfamadore with a bunch of creatures shaped like toilet plungers.

> **Barbara Pilgrim**: I thought we talked about this.
>
> **Billy**: What is it about this that makes you so mad?
>
> **Barbara**: None of it's true! There is no such planet!
>
> **Billy**: It can't be detected from Earth, if that's what you mean.

● **Barbara** isn't sure what to do with her father.

> **Billy**: I'm unstuck in time.
>
> **Barbara**: Is that so.
>
> **Billy**: Yes, in fact, I was just at a banquet for your brother's Little League team. Before that I was in a forest in World War II. Then I was back in the womb.
>
> **Barbara**: Please don't lie to me.
>
> **Kurt Vonnegut**: This was a fairly pretty girl, except that she had legs like an Edwardian grand piano.
>
> **Barbara**: What's going on?
>
> **Kurt Vonnegut**: Barbara is a bitchy flibbertigibbet.
>
> **Barbara**: I'm going to log off for a while.

● **Billy** is drunk in the backseat of his car.

✉ **Billy** sent a **Tell Me Where My Steering Wheel Is So I Can Drive Home** request.

Billy received a **Standing Ovation** from the **Lions Club**.

 Billy added **Frozen European Creek Bed in World War II** to his **Places I Didn't Plan on Visiting**.

 Billy received **The Crap Beat Out of Him** from **Roland Weary**.

Billy is as rich as Croesus.

Billy removed "staying awake during patient visits at my optometry office" from his **Activities**.

The Germans added **Billy** to their **Prisoners of War**.

Billy became a fan of **"Magic Fingers" Bed-Vibrator Machines**.

? **Billy** took a **What Kind of Earthling Are You?** quiz with the result "Fine Specimen."

Billy is nestled like spoons with a hobo.

Billy saw the late movie backwards, then forwards again.

Billy added "If you're ever in Cody, Wyoming, just ask for Wild Bob!" to his **Favorite Quotations**.

Kurt Vonnegut added "So it goes" to his **Effective Rhetorical Devices**.

The Germans sent **Billy** a **Coat That's More Like a Three-Cornered Hat with Gummy Stains and a Dead, Furry Animal Frozen to It**.

Billy says that to the Tralfamadorians, the heavens look like they're filled with rarefied, luminous spaghetti.

Billy added "have spent time as a Nonviolent Mental Patient" to his **About Me**.

Billy is twelve years old, terrified, and standing at the rim of the Grand Canyon.

Billy is being deloused.

Billy is attending **The Saddest-Ever Version of Cinderella**.

 Billy received **His Own Time of Death**.

> **Kurt Vonnegut**: So it goes.

 Billy became a fan of **Kilgore Trout**.

 Billy is now married to **Valencia Merble**.

 Valencia Merble joined the group **Women with Carbon Monoxide Intolerance**.

> **Kurt Vonnegut**: So it goes.

● **Billy** is loony with time travel and morphine.

 Billy received a **Mating** request from **Montana Wildhack**, motion picture star.

● **Billy** is being patronized by a Blue Fairy Godmother.

● **Billy** took a leak in the simulated earthling habitat of the Tralfamadorian zoo. The crowd went wild.

> **Barbara**: Did you hear what I said? If you're going to act like a child, maybe we'll just have to treat you like a child.
>
> **Billy**: That isn't what happens next.
>
> **Barbara**: We'll see what happens next.

● **Billy** is leading a sad parade of American prisoners through the streets of Dresden wearing a blue toga and silver shoes, with his hands in a muff.

● **Billy** is boarding a plane that he knows is going to crash, but he doesn't want to make a fool of himself by saying so.

● **Billy** added "Making (while eating a lot of) malt syrup" to his **Activities**.

● **Billy** is now friends with **Kilgore Trout**.

- **Billy** is crying his eyes out at a barbershop quartet.

- **Billy** is attending the **Bombing of Dresden via Meat Locker**.

- **Billy** does not have echolalia.

- **Billy** is snoozing in the back of a wagon.

- **Billy** suddenly wants to tell the world the lessons he learned on Tralfamadore.

- **Barbara** is putting Billy to bed and turning on the Magic Fingers.

  > **Barbara**: Don't go anywhere, Dad.

- **Billy** is sneaking out and going to New York to go on the radio and tell the world about Tralfamadore.

- **Billy** posted a **Note**.

  > —*I'm going to die February 13, 1976. So it goes.*

  > —*That's okay—to the Tralfamadorians, it's just one moment in time and I'll still be alive elsewhere.*

  > —*The Tralfamadorians ignore the awful times and concentrate on the good ones.*

- **Kurt Vonnegut** is grateful, then, that so many of his moments are nice.

- **Billy** was told that Tralfamadorian novels are a series of urgent messages with no particular relationship to each other that when seen all at once make something beautiful.

- **Kurt Vonnegut** wrote a Tralfamadorian novel.

- **Kurt Vonnegut** is not a fan of **War**.

- **Kurt Vonnegut** said at the start of his story that there's nothing to say about a massacre, when everything is supposed to be quiet, except for the birds that say "Poo-tee-weet?"

- **Billy** woke up one day in Dresden, and World War II was over.

  > **A Bird**: Poo-tee-weet?

Waiting for Godot
NEWS FEED

● **Estragon** is trying to take his boot off.

> **Jean-Paul Sartre**: Oh, I get it! Life is absurd!

📄 **Estragon** shared a **Conversation About the Gospels** with **Vladimir**.

> **Søren Kierkegaard**: It's about God! God is Godot!
>
> **Vladimir**: That's who we're waiting for.
>
> **Estragon**: We are? Why can't we go?
>
> **Vladimir**: We're waiting for Godot.
>
> **Søren Kierkegaard**: God!
>
> **Vladimir**: Godot.

● **Estragon** and **Vladimir** are not sure they're in the right place.

> **Albert Camus**: Life is confusing!
>
> **Estragon**: What did we do yesterday?
>
> **Vladimir**: What did we do yesterday?
>
> **Albert Camus**: And repetitive! Life is repetitive! Isn't it repetitive?

● **Estragon** thinks maybe they should erase their accounts.

● **Estragon** wonders but what if only one of them erases his account and the other is online alone?

> **Sigmund Freud**: Ah, you're talking about human relationships!
>
> **Estragon**: And we?
>
> **Vladimir**: I beg your pardon?

Estragon: I said, "And we?"

Vladimir: I don't understand.

Sigmund Freud: Yes, yes, you're like a married couple!

Vladimir sent **Estragon** a **Carrot**.

Vladimir: How's the carrot?

Estragon: It's a carrot.

Sigmund Freud: Hmmm.

Pozzo sent **Estragon** some **Chicken Bones**.

Søren Kierkegaard: Death! Christ! No, that tree is Christ. A tree of life! A cross!

Pozzo asked Estragon his name, and he answered "Adam."

Søren Kierkegaard: See? God! The Bible! They're all of humanity! They're people!

Lucky can only think with his hat on.

Albert Camus: Humanity! Hats! Oh, he's Charlie Chaplin!

Jean-Paul Sartre: They're vaudeville. They're representing human history. And the history of theatre!

Albert Camus: And hats!

Lucky is thinking out loud.

Lucky received a **Full-Body Tackle** from **Estragon**, **Vladimir**, and **Pozzo**.

Franz Kafka: Ooof, the pain, when you try to think out loud and they punish you!

Pozzo is trampling Lucky's hat.

Søren Kierkegaard: Buster Keaton? And God!

Pozzo is explaining the twilight.

Albert Camus: Distraction! Life needs distraction!

A boy wrote on **Vladimir's** and **Estragon's Walls**.

"Godot isn't coming today, but he will tomorrow."

Estragon dedicated "Should I Stay or Should I Go" to **Vladimir**.

> **Jean-Paul Sartre**: Aha! No exit! The world is so absurd!

Estragon thinks we should go.

Vladimir is agreeing.

Estragon and **Vladimir** are not leaving.

Vladimir thinks he and Estragon need each other.

> **Sigmund Freud**: Ah, you're an id and an ego!

Pozzo is now blind and running into Lucky and falling down.

> **James Joyce**: You're Jungian! You're the Cold War! You're England and Ireland! You're Oedipal!
>
> **Oedipus**: What?

Pozzo sent a **Help** request.

Estragon and **Vladimir** are discussing at length whether or not to help him.

> **Hamlet**: Our human futility! We spend too much time talking and not doing.
>
> **Vladimir**: Let us do something while we have the chance!
>
> **Hamlet**: SEE?
>
> **Jean-Paul Sartre**: It seems to be about the not-doing though. It's a whole play where nothing happens.
>
> **Jerry Seinfeld**: Is there anything wrong with that?

Vladimir tried to help Pozzo and fell down.

- **Estragon** tried to help Vladimir and fell down.

  Albert Camus: Oh, we're useless, useless humans! We try to help and we just fail. We're Sisyphean!

- **Estragon** is referring to Pozzo as "Cain" and "Abel."

  Søren Kierkegaard: GOD! Godot! God!

  Vladimir: Don't leave me!

  Pozzo: Where am I?

  Estragon: Who farted?

  Falstaff: That happens!

- **Pozzo** and **Lucky** are leaving again.

- **Estragon** received **Pain** from his **Feet**.

  Franz Kafka: Feet! Oh, the pain of being human!

- **Vladimir** thinks habit is a great deadener.

  Albert Camus: SISYPHUS!

  Odysseus: Where?

- **The boy** reposted yesterday's **message** on **Vladimir's** and **Estragon's Walls**.

  "Godot isn't coming today, but he will tomorrow."

- **Estragon** wonders if they should hang themselves.

  Albert Camus: Death! Futility! Chicken bones! Carrots!

- **Estragon** says we can bring rope tomorrow.

  Hamlet: Don't do it! Or maybe you should! Or not.

● **Vladimir** is telling Estragon to pull up his pants.

> **Franz Kafka**: So true! My pants are always falling down!

● **Vladimir** thinks they should go.

> **Jean-Paul Sartre**: It's existential! It's life!
>
> **Søren Kierkegaard**: It's waiting for death! And God!
>
> **Hamlet**: And theatre!
>
> **Albert Camus**: It's religion and humanity and war!
>
> **Sigmund Freud**: And the human mind!
>
> **Jerry Seinfeld**: And entertainment!
>
> **Albert Camus**: And the absurd! Isn't it? Isn't it?
>
> **Samuel Beckett**: Whatever.

● **Estragon** is agreeing.

● **Vladimir** and **Estragon** are not leaving.

James Joyce, William Faulkner, and Ernest Hemingway Play Scrabulific!

R	A	I	N	
	D			
	Z			W
M	E	I	S	E
U				N
C				T
H				
S				
I				
A	H	U	N	
S				

SMACK TALK!

Hemingway: I'm getting very tired of this. I don't understand why you both keep making up words.

Joyce: What are you talking about?

Hemingway: *Meise?* What's a meise?

Joyce: A meise, you know, a meise. The animal. As in, as sautril as a meise.

Hemingway: See, those aren't real words.

Joyce: Sure they are. It's all about context. You put anything in context and people will know what you're talking about.

Hemingway: Okay, but this context is Scrabulific, and you can only use words that EXIST.

Joyce: I'm not getting you. Of course, these words exist. And they're a lot more interesting than *went*. What is that about? You want to put people to sleep?

Faulkner: Clearly, he does.

Hemingway: I'm not talking to you, Chick-fil-A. *Ahun* and *adze*?? My adze.

Joyce: See, you just did it, you put it in context!

Faulkner: Yes, but an adze isn't an ass. It's actually in the dictionary. Not that Ernie has ever had to go near one. Or any of his readers.

Hemingway: Enough with that joke! And really that's what we want for our readers, to have to sit there with footnotes and reference materials just to get through a page?

Joyce: Of course.

Faulkner: Clearly.

Hemingway: And what the hell is *muchsias*??

Joyce: You know, *muchsias*, or "thanks." Like muschsias grapcias.

Hemingway: That does not count.

Joyce: Yes it does, I have 157 points. And you have 4.

Hemingway: That's not right at all.

Faulkner: May I have 6,700 more points? And a bottle ot scotch? And a trIple word score?

Joyce: My pleasure.

Faulkner: Muchsias grapcias my sautril little meise.

Hemingway: I hate you.

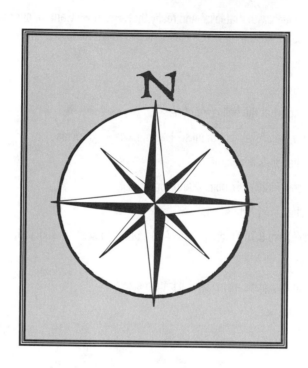

9

F. Scott Fitzgerald beat on, a boat against the current, borne back ceaselessly into the past.

Notes

Maidens Who Don't Float • Famous Last Words

Maidens Who Don't Float

PROFILE

Basic Information

Networks: Everywhere

Favorite Music: "Everyday I Write the Book," "I Could Write a Book," "The Book of Love"

Friends

William Shakespeare, Homer, Geoffrey Chaucer, Dante Alighieri, John Milton, Unknown, Jane Austen, Charlotte Brontë, Emily Brontë, Leo Tolstoy, Nathaniel Hawthorne, Mark Twain, Harper Lee, Charles Dickens, J. D. Salinger, Louisa May Alcott, Lewis Carroll, Herman Melville, Jonathan Swift, Ernest Hemingway, Aldous Huxley, George Orwell, Margaret Mitchell, William Golding, Miguel de Cervantes, Fyodor Dostoyevsky, Thomas Pynchon, Victor Hugo, Joseph Conrad, Edgar Allan Poe, Franz Kafka, Mary Shelley, Robert Louis Stevenson, Bram Stoker, Vladimir Nabokov, D. H. Lawrence, Oscar Wilde, Sophocles, John Steinbeck, Arthur Miller, F. Scott Fitzgerald, Edith Wharton, Jack Kerouac, William Faulkner, Virginia Woolf, James Joyce, Kurt Vonnegut, Samuel Beckett [and many more]

Groups

Member of:

Maidens Who Don't Float; I Was a Preteen Bride; Keeping the Tempted in Unattempted; The Original Naturists; That's Nice You Made a Whole Movie About It, But I Hardly Knew Tom Lefroy; Famous Governesses of the World Who Love Their Masters, Even If It Bucks Societal Norms; Kings of France Who Don't Speak French; Dukes Who Hawk Tartar-Takin'-Off Remedies; Males Who Should Keep Their Hair and Whiskers as Short as Possible; I Secretly Want to Punch Anyone Inferior to Me in the Back of the Head; Maidens Who Are Not Inflammable; Men Who Don't Float (Unless They Happen to Find a Coffin-Shaped Buoy); I Could Eat a Year's Worth of Your Food in Five Seconds; Humankind; Americans Who Join the Italian Army Because They Happen to Be in Italy; The Italian Army; All My Homes Are Now Museums; Breeders of Six-Toed Cats; Intoxicated Important American Writers; Intoxicated Nobel Laureates; The Confederate Army; The USA; The Flies' Twentieth Reunion!; Killers Who Are Doing It Just for Fun Now; People with Obsessive-Compulsive Disorder; People with Batty Murderess

Sleepwalking Disorder; Yeah, I'm a Loser, and What Literary Genres Have YOU Started?; The Undead; Sane People Who Happen to Live in a Mental Hospital; The Dead Dead; Men Who Should Have Used Protection; Men Who Might Be Found Wandering Around Sick and Delirious in Someone Else's Clothes; Maidens Who Should Avoid Catching Cold with All That Tuberculosis Going Around; Men Who Are Not Bulletproof; Women Not Good with Mercury; People Who Shouldn't Leave Their Wives at Age Eighty-Two and Go Traveling; Men Who Should Have Joined the Group Alcoholics Anonymous; People Who Probably Should Stop the Nonstop Speaking Engagements After Surviving That Horrific Train Crash; People Who Come and Go with Halley's Comet; People Who Really Shouldn't Keep a Journal; Women Not Able to Stop Moving Vehicles with Themselves; King Loopy and His Freaks of Nature; People Who Had No Chance of Surviving Shakespeare's Most Depressing Tragedy; Women Who Don't Defy Gravity; Men Who Shouldn't Drive at the End of a Tragedy; Obvious Racists; Men Who Float But Are Still Not Impervious to Bullets; Former High-Society Women Ill-Equipped to Make Hats; Some of My Ancestors Were Killed in Duels; Nobel Laureates Who Didn't Go to College; Oxford Men; Yes I Wrote It That Way Just to Mess with You; Chronological Order Is for Sissies; SAVE WATER . . . Drink Whiskey; Important Southern Writers; Bloomsbury; Women with Carbon Monoxide Intolerance

Applications

Places I've Been; Places I Want to Visit; Choose a Good Husband!; War on All Y'all; Violent British Children; Speaking Her Mind; Marrying Someone Out of Pure Spite; Emily Brontë's Brain-Numbingly Similar Name Generator; Fathering a Frail Wimpy Son; Payback Time; Build Your Own Raft; Moral Quandary; Bogus Scams; Inciting Bloodthirsty Uprisings; Worst-Ever Fake British Accents; Rob a Dead Man; Fits and Starts of War; Horse-Riding; Gettin' Revenge 'n Protectin' the Women; Be a Sweet and True Woman; Man Up Already; Second Life; Infantilizing a Wealthy Gentleman; Gradually Increasing Husband-Hatred; Ocular Digging; Pleading the Fifth; I'm the King and I'm Charging You with Murder If You Won't Tell Us Who the Murderer Is; Obviously Abandoned Baby Detector; Family Tree Fun!; Think Up a Useless Idea That Isn't Going to Help Anyone; Having a Breakdown in Real Time; Third Wheel; Sleep; Sweet-Moment Interrupter; Tell Your Wife You Love Her

Fan Pages

Daggers; Using Sex to Lord Over My Husband(s); Men in Military Uniform Like Mr. Wickham; Clueless; SWEET REVENGE; YOU DON'T KNOW SWEET REVENGE UNTIL YOU SEE THIS KIND OF REVENGE REVENGE; Necrophilia; Needlework; Outkast; Angels; Breaking and Entering, But Only in a Romantic Convoluted Way Like is the Custom in Europe by the Best Authorities in Writin' Novels; The Grudge; Mean Girls; There Will Be Blood; The Tudors; Blatant Foreshadowing; Sperm; Men; Excrement; Cognac; Brandy; Sherry; Grappa; Wine; Using a Neutral Disinterested Tone to Heighten the Realism of War; Detachment; Stoicism; Aloofness; Not Fighting in Wars; Loving Anyone Ever; The Bulls;

The Spanish Inquisition; Garbage; Weird Science; Wedding Crashers; The Carpathian Mountains; Spiders; Flies; Sparrows; Sleepwalking; Sewage; Girls My Age if This Was Twenty-Five Years Ago; Functional Motels; Man-Friends; Driving the Point Home or So to Speak; Curley's Wife's Hair; Giant Contradictions; Fairly Obvious But Eloquently Written Metaphors; Dr. T. J. Eckleburg's Optical Emporium; Gambling; Sleep Medication; Poison; Yoknapatawpha County; Owning a Room; "Magic Fingers" Bed-Vibrator Machines; Kilgore Trout

Famous Last Words

NEWS FEED

- **Charles Dickens** has done a far, far better thing that he does, than he has ever done; it is a far, far better rest that he goes to than he has ever known.

- **Charles Dickens** saw no shadow of another parting from her.

- **Charles Dickens** observed, God Bless Us, Every One!

- **F. Scott Fitzgerald** beat on, a boat against the current, borne back ceaselessly into the past.

- **Ernest Hemingway** went out and left the hospital and walked back to the hotel in the rain.

- **Ernest Hemingway** is dreaming about the lions.

  > **Ernest Hemingway**: Isn't it pretty to think so?

- **Mark Twain** can't stand it. He's been there before.

- **Margaret Mitchell** will think of some way to get him back. After all, tomorrow is another day.

- **George Orwell** loved Big Brother.

- **Jack Kerouac** thinks of Dean Moriarty.

- **Emily Brontë** wondered how anyone could ever imagine unquiet slumbers for the sleepers in that quiet earth.

- **William Faulkner** doesn't! He doesn't! He doesn't hate it! He doesn't hate it!

- **Lewis Carroll** is remembering his own child-life, and the happy summer days.

- **Willa Cather** possessed together the precious, the incommunicable past.

- **John Milton,** with wandering steps and slow, through Eden took his solitary way.

- **Herman Melville** only found another orphan.

- **Mary Shelley** was soon borne away by the waves and lost in darkness and distance.

- **Harper Lee** would be there when Jem waked up in the morning.

- **Vladimir Nabokov** is the only immortality you and I may share, my Lolita.

- **Gustave Flaubert** has just received the cross of the Legion of Honor.

- **Zora Neale Hurston** called in her soul to come and see.

- **Louisa May Alcott** never can wish you a greater happiness than this!

- **L. Frank Baum** is so glad to be at home again.

- **Jane Austen** was ever sensible of the warmest gratitude towards the persons who, by bringing her into Derbyshire, had been the means of uniting them.

- **Saul Bellow** had no messages for anyone. Nothing. Not a single word.

- **Jack London,** at the instant he knew, he ceased to know.

- **Richard Wright** heard the ring of steel against steel as a far door clanged shut.

- **John Steinbeck's** lips came together and smiled mysteriously.

- **John Steinbeck's** eyes closed and he slept.

- **William Golding** is allowing his eyes to rest on the trim cruiser in the distance.

- **Ray Bradbury** stared back up at them for a long, long silent time from the rippling water.

- **Haruki Murakami** drifted off for a moment.

   > **Toni Morrison**: Look where your hands are. Now.
   >
   > **Thomas Pynchon**: Now everybody—
   >
   > **Philip Roth**: Now vee may perhaps to begin. Yes?

- **Joseph Heller** took off.

- **Robert Louis Stevenson** has the sharp voice of Captain Flint still ringing in his ears: "Pieces of eight! Pieces of eight!"

- **Albert Camus** had only to wish that there be a large crowd of spectators the day of his execution and that they greet him with cries of hate.

- **Kurt Vonnegut** said to Billy Pilgrim, "Poo-tee-weet?"

- **Homer** ended the strife forever.

- **Daniel Defoe** is now worth 800 pounds, but shall never be so happy, as when he was not worth a farthing.

- **Thomas Hardy** arose, joined hands again, and went on.

   > **Thomas Hardy**: It might have been worse, and I feel my thanks accordingly.

- **Leo Tolstoy's** whole life, regardless of all that may happen to him, every minute of it, is not only not meaningless, as it was before, but has the unquestionable meaning of the good which it is in his power to put into it!

- **J. D. Salinger** says don't ever tell anybody anything. If you do, you start missing everybody.

- **E. M. Forster** heard the river, bearing down the snows of winter into the Mediterranean.

- **D. H. Lawrence** walked towards the faintly humming, glowing town, quickly.

- **A. A. Milne,** wherever he goes, and whatever happens to him on the way, in that enchanted place on top of the Forest, a little boy and his Bear will always be playing.

- **Sylvia Plath** stepped into the room.

- **Virginia Woolf** had her vision.

- **James Joyce** a way a lone a last a loved a long the

- **Henry James** shall never be again as we were!

- **Raymond Chandler** never saw her again.

- **Fyodor Dostoyevsky's** present story is ended.

> **Fyodor Dostoyevsky**: It seems that this will be a good place to stop.
>
> **Margaret Atwood**: Are there any questions?
>
> **William Makepeace Thackeray**: Let us shut up the box and the puppets, for our play is played out.
>
> **Miguel de Cervantes**: Farewell.
>
> **Norman Mailer**: TO BE CONTINUED
>
> **Graham Greene**: Leave me alone forever.
>
> **Gabriel García Márquez**: "Forever," he said.
>
> **Don DeLillo**: Peace.
>
> **William Shakespeare**: Exeunt.